Forgiveness

Your Key to Harmony
and Inner Peace

A M e m o i r

by

Laura Throne

Tellwell Talent
www.tellwell.ca

ISBN
978-0-2288-2446-6 (Hardcover)
978-0-2288-2445-9 (Paperback)
978-0-2288-2447-3 (eBook)

Author's Note

This memoir is a recollection of events in the author's life. The information contained in this memoir is true and complete to the best of the author's knowledge. The names and identifying characteristics of individuals have been changed to maintain anonymity and protect their privacy. It is not the author's intention to inflict any harm on any individual in publishing this memoir. The events, places and conversations in this memoir have been recreated from memory, and the chronology of some events has been compressed.

This book does not provide, and does not intend to provide, medical advice of any kind. The information in this book is not a substitute for professional medical advice, and a medical professional should be consulted before following any information or exercise in this book. Any questions or concerns regarding your health, wellbeing, and safety should be discussed with healthcare professionals. The author does not assume any responsibility for any loss, injury, claim, liability, or damage related to your use of this book.

Table of Contents

Dedication

This book is dedicated to my amazing grandma, my helpful mom and my precious children. It is also dedicated to Margaret, who supported me on the way.

I also dedicate this book to all women who make our world a better place with their kindness, compassion and powerful inner wisdom.

Finally, this book is dedicated to those who have hurt someone or have been hurt by someone and are now ready to find forgiveness.

Introduction

"The weak can never forgive.
Forgiveness is the attribute of the strong."
Mahatma Gandhi

We often look for explanations of why certain events we consider negative or "bad luck" (i.e., an accident, financial disaster, loss of job, sickness or failure of a marriage) happened to us. We want to understand the unfortunate situation with our minds; we seek reason. We often blame ourselves or others for our problems and difficulties. *Why me?* Sometimes there is no explanation. We just have to trust the Universe that everything happens for our best and highest interest. We need to believe that in the end all will work out wonderfully for us, even if we don't see the *"how"* or understand the *"why."*

In my life I have asked these questions repeatedly: Why did this happen to me? Why do I have to face so many obstacles and challenges? Why is my life full of emotional struggles and physical pain? Why did I feel miserable, helpless and unhappy for so many years?

I searched for answers unsuccessfully for a long time. Now I know the answers to all those questions and many others. Even if I don't understand every aspect of what takes place in my life, I accept it; I no longer blame myself and others for these events. I know in my heart that everything — even the negative experiences — happen for a reason. It all serves my best interest and supports my spiritual and personal growth. It is also important to believe in yourself and trust you can do it. When you truly believe in yourself, the impossible becomes possible. For example, at the age of twenty-four I hardly spoke English; now I'm writing and publishing my book in English. Learning to believe in myself and my potential has served me well.

I hope you find answers to some of your questions in this book, and that you also learn to accept that sometimes trusting yourself and the universal consciousness is more important than finding explanations for everything in your life. It is crucial to keep an open mind and understand that there is something bigger and greater than us. I call this Universe, God/Goddess, higher consciousness, and collective or universal consciousness. Once you open your mind to new information and perspectives and learn how to connect to the universal consciousness and your higher self, the quality of your life will improve significantly. Your *higher self* (some call it spirit) is connected to the universal consciousness and resides in another dimension (not in the physical realm and it is not affected by your physical reality). Your higher self is the pure essence of you. Your soul, on the other hand, incarnates into this body to experience all the physical, emotional and mental challenges on Earth. Your higher self has answers to all your questions therefore it is crucial to find the connection. Once you do, you begin living your life easily and effortlessly. You find the harmony, love, joy, peace and balance you have been searching for all your life.

I share how I have found my inner peace and happiness and set my soul free through forgiveness and my spiritual awakening process. My life is proof that forgiveness is possible even after the most desperate, hopeless and miserable marriage, and difficult life situations such as my chronic disease and multiple surgeries. I truly believe that I was inspired by Higher Realms to share my story with the world, spread the message of forgiveness and lift human consciousness. It is fascinating how the whole Universe has helped me complete my book.

My memoir is a true story. Everything happened the way I describe it. I have included significant experiences and important events of my life, but it by no means covers everything. I have changed the necessary details to protect the identity of my family and my ex-husband. It is not my intention to offend him, ruin his reputation or retaliate. We all make mistakes. We all have different challenges in life and various lessons to learn. I won't judge anybody's journey, including my ex-husband's. I have forgiven him for all he has done, and I have no intention to hurt him.

That said, the parts of his life that intersect with mine become a part of my story; I cannot write about one without the other, and so he must play a role in the pages that follow. Therefore, I have changed his name, our children's names, and I have chosen to write under a pen name. I neither identify the company he has worked for, nor specify countries where we lived. The only country I identify where we lived, and I currently reside, is Canada.

In the last fifteen years I have lived in four countries on three continents, and I have visited many amazing places all over the world. I have been exposed to diverse cultures, languages, religions, traditions and cuisines. I have met the poorest of the poor and the richest of the rich. The difference between the quality of life in these countries is appalling. People living in the

West can't imagine the scale of poverty and hunger many people face in developing countries. On the other hand, people living in extreme poverty who lack food, water and shelter can't envision a life of large houses and expensive cars, or even reliable healthcare and good education systems. I have seen the two extremes of the spectrum. The gap is widening between the richest and the poorest in developed countries as well. Division between the small percentage of rich and high percentage of poor with a declining middle class is significant in some Western countries. Wealth is unequally distributed and there are huge inequalities.

Despite our economic differences and diverse religions, languages and cultures, we all want the same thing: freedom, happiness, peace, good health, love, security and a meaningful, fulfilling and rewarding life. We also all experience despair, sickness, pain, unhappiness, anger, anxiety, sadness and fear. Although our life experiences and circumstances are very different, deep down we are the same. Although we experience separation from each other on Earth, we are all connected.

Each of us has a story and all of us are presented with challenges and difficulties in life — some are bigger, some are smaller, but they are always significant. I'm not here to teach you anything. I am simply sharing experiences and life lessons from my spiritual journey to show you how I chose to respond. I have included practical information you can use when facing difficult life situations, and it is up to you how much you use from this book, if anything.

I will share some of my thoughts about marriage and how important it is to make conscious and informed decisions by following our intuition and feelings. Fear and uncertainty often hold us back from achieving our true potential and finding our happiness. Women in distressed, unloving and humiliating marriages can find their inner power and strength by getting rid of their fear and leaving their comfort zone behind. Deep down, you know what is good for you. Even if you think you don't have a choice or there are only bad choices, think again. You always have a choice and you are the only one who knows what the best decision is for you in a particular situation. You possess all the wisdom you need. If you make your decisions intentionally and consciously by following your inner voice and your heart, you will come to the best outcome. You can either stay in that relationship or leave. Once you decide to take a different path and take control over your life, you will be so strong and empowered that nobody can stop you. You will also find all the resources and support you need to take actions. I will show you how the Universe will reward you and take care of you when you step into the unknown and embrace change.

By strengthening your self-love and self-acceptance and eliminating your fears you become stronger and more confident about who you are and what you are capable of. Remember: you are worthy and powerful! You have all the wisdom you need to make conscious decisions about changes in your life that will achieve balance and harmony emotionally, physically, mentally and spiritually.

Gratitude and kindness are critical in everybody's life. Accept everything that life offers with gratitude. Generosity and gentleness can transform our lives. You've probably heard about the law of Karma — cause and effect or what you give out, you get back. Even if you don't believe in Karma, you still can live your life with kindness by reaching out to people in need and helping our planet, nature and animals. At the end of the day we are all connected, and our lives are deeply intertwined through millions of invisible threads.

I will talk about how my chronic disease and my near-death experience changed my life and started my spiritual journey, which resulted in the search for my purpose and destiny. I also describe all the details of my lifestyle changes that restored my emotional and physical health.

Finally, I share my thoughts about how important it is to live in the present moment instead of always reliving past hurt or planning our happiness in the future. Talking about negative past events, thinking about unhappy moments and complaining about people who damaged us or hurt our family will not solve our problems; rather, it will prolong our helplessness and negative feelings in the now. It will also fill our life with anger, stress, worry and resentment. These emotions can decrease our vitality and sometimes can cause physical disease, as has been my case. So, whenever we are ready, it is better to release those past events and forgive ourselves and those people the feelings are associated with.

Forgiveness can change everything and everyone in this world. Forgiveness is neither about the other person nor about forgetting the past; rather, it is something you give to yourself to find inner peace and harmony in life. One must be very strong and committed to forgive. Forgiving ourselves is just as important as forgiving others. We have to forgive ourselves and the people who have hurt us. There is no right or wrong way to go. If we feel stuck and overwhelmed by anger, fear or grief, prayers can always help us overcome those negative feelings. Emotional, physical, and mental healing takes time. Some wounds are too deep; therefore, finding forgiveness can take years for some people and it can take months for others. It can't be forced; it comes naturally when we are ready, but we must be committed and persistent.

Sometimes it seems almost impossible to let go of the past. We have to. It is the only way that will ultimately free us and give us what we desire most: peace. We have to let go of our anger, blame, guilt, resentment and all the negative emotions we carry in our heart from the past. Angels reminded me to include the fact that no matter how big or how small our "mistakes" and "faults" may be, we can always ask for forgiveness. Once we leave this world, we will be the only judge of our actions as we look back on our lives and go through our "life review." Nobody will judge us. Don't be afraid to ask for forgiveness and offer forgiveness. If a person you need to forgive has passed away or lives far away from you, visualize her or him in your mind and ask for forgiveness and give forgiveness. There are different techniques and excellent exercises that can help you in this process.

Some people can never forgive and end up leaving this world with hatred, bitterness, guilt and negative emotions in their hearts. Please don't be one of them. Don't leave this world feeling upset and resentful with your spouse, children, boss, friends, parents, neighbours, business partners, etc. — yourself. We need to find true forgiveness in our hearts and transform our world.

After reading my book you might rethink your relationships and life and decide to free yourself from anger, resentment, worry, stress and fear. Your life will become peaceful, calm, joyous and filled with love and kindness. All you have to do is forgive and be kind to yourself and others.

Reading my memoir and other spiritual books will assist you on your path. Your heart and your higher self will guide you to finding your harmony, balance and purpose on Earth.

Chapter One

My Childhood

I love water — it feels like home to me. It is one of the four fundamental elements: air, water, fire, earth. Water means life: it is essential for all living beings to survive. Most of the human body, just like our Earth, is comprised of water.

In astrology, water represents feelings and emotions. I was born under a water sign, which means I am a very emotional being with highly tuned intuition. I'm sensitive and deeply passionate. Spending time near the sea, a river, a lake or a swimming pool helps me release tension and stress. I like floating on the surface of the water with my eyes closed. I feel free and incredibly light as the water holds me up. It's like my problems are washing away as I surrender. Interestingly, all of the significant and sometimes scary experiences I describe in this book are somehow related to water. Here's the first one.

I grew up in a little village in Europe. When I was nine or ten, my family went on holiday overseas with several other families. It was so lovely to spend the days playing in the fragrant spring tulips, violets and poppies, and basking in the sun.

One day, my brother and his friends discovered a passage that was across a rushing river — one of those rivers you would go rafting on, very fast. The banks were steep and a thin tree that had fallen was the only means to cross it. They were very excited to show what they had found, so they rushed across on the tree and disappeared into the forest on the other side. As I hastily tried to keep up, my pants got tangled up on a branch, I lost my balance and plunged deep into the river. The water rushed by incredibly fast and should have dragged me with it, but it didn't. I stayed in the same spot where I fell. No matter how strong the water flow was and how light my body was, I did not move. In a way, I was hovering, but I could "breathe." I was not gasping for air; I was very peaceful and calm. I had no fear whatsoever. I knew I was safe and going to be OK. When I opened my eyes under water, I saw lots of long, green weeds around me. My mother was just behind us and she jumped into the river after me. She fiercely swam against the strong current and eventually plucked me out of the threatening waters. I don't know how long I stayed under water but I was absolutely fine after getting out of the river.

I'm sure many people have similar experiences and "accidents" as children when they were miraculously saved. These memories stick with you because they are special. Perhaps we forget a lot about our childhood and school, but an experience like this stays with us for decades.

Why was I saved?

Why wasn't I swept away and drowned?

It is easy to answer: it was not my time yet.

I have mixed memories about my childhood: happiness and calm disrupted by fights with my dad. My father was good looking, tall and thin when he was young. He was well-educated, with a university degree in engineering. He always drank a lot and was verbally abusive when he was drunk. He screamed a lot at my mom, my brother and me. As a child I was really scared of him. It was emotionally exhausting and draining being around him. He never showed me the love or attention I longed for. He could not take any criticism, but he was very critical of everyone else. He thought he was special and the world revolved around him. Everyone had to "serve" him, admire him and pay attention to him when he talked. He controlled my mother's life and often humiliated her. He was an executive director at a medium size company and made good money. Earning money and establishing financial security was his way to show "love" toward his family. With time he gained a lot of weight, lost his hair and paid no attention to his body. Now he is extremely overweight and in very poor health.

My mother was stunning when she married my father. She had a beautiful face with a perfect nose and lips, along with big blue eyes. She has always been skinny. After forty years working in a kindergarten, she managed a restaurant and banquet hall where she hosted big wedding parties and events. She worked hard and relentlessly her whole life, which meant she never had much time for my brother and me. She juggled her full-time job at the kindergarten, household chores and later her extra job in the restaurant in addition to looking after her own children. She tried to "do it all," and it was too much for her. It would have been too much for anyone. My mom had lots of energy. She was always on the move and doing something. She could not slow down or enjoy the moment, and she lived her life as a big "drama." She enjoyed complaining and judging other people. I used to be like her.

She was an excellent cook. We always had delicious four-course lunches on Sundays. I loved those family meals. We ate chicken soup with lots of noodles and vegetables, followed by a special cherry sauce. We had chicken or sausage with potatoes as the main course followed by delicious homemade desserts. My mother made these dishes effortlessly. I didn't know at the time how long it takes to prepare a meal like this and how much labour everyday cooking and baking is.

She did not show me love in the way I needed. She was not very affectionate and did not hug me often. I remember the bliss of lying next to her in bed at night. I know she loved and loves me very much, but I did not feel it as a child. Now I know she did the best she could as a mother. We all do. I can't think of anybody else in my life who has been more helpful than my mother. She was the only person to always be there for me. For that I'm eternally grateful.

My mom did her best to protect us from my father's anger and rage. She quietly suffered a lot and made tremendous efforts to keep peace in the family. My father treated her as a "servant." This is not an isolated case. In my opinion lots of men in traditional societies still think the woman's main job is to raise children and do household chores. This outdated notion is evolving, but it is still dominant in some societies and many families. Of course, there is a long history in regard to a woman's "inferior" status to a man in every area of life. The long process of the liberation of women and achieving equal rights to men is not yet finished. A woman's list of household chores can be incredibly long. Cooking, cleaning, baking, grocery shopping, doing laundry and dishes, and childcare is a full-time job. It is an exhausting, thankless job that pays nothing. It is unfortunate that some men like my father don't appreciate the work women do every day.

There are encouraging and inspiring signs in some countries — especially in Canada and the Nordic countries — that women have broken free from these obsolete roles and earned more power and responsibility in politics, economics, and financial and healthcare sectors outside their "traditional" roles, but significantly *more* needs to be done. Women need to step up and meaningfully influence every area of our lives, especially in arenas such as politics, finance and science. This will ultimately create a better place for our children and for our environment.

I loved Christmas as a child: decorating the tree, preparing gifts for everyone (my grandmother taught me how to sew and helped me prepare Christmas gifts) and breathlessly waiting to unwrap what was under the tree was a special experience. My grandmother always came to our place for lunch, and the next day we went to the church together. As children we played a lot together, but I haven't been very close to my brother as we've become adults. I grew up with my cousin who lived in the house next door and spent my childhood with her. Later we drifted apart as I lived in different countries for many years. Interestingly, we now live in the same neighbourhood, so we often see each other.

I spent every summer holiday with my brother and my cousin at my grandmother's house. As children we did not do any organized sports or creative activities like most kids do nowadays, nor did we have many toys and games. Most of the day we were outside in the garden. My grandmother had a huge garden with raspberries, strawberries, apple and cherry trees, and all sorts of vegetables like potatoes, peas, peppers and tomatoes. We ate everything off the trees and bushes. She even had poppies in her garden. I remember her cutting off the top of the poppies and drying them out in the sun. Then she baked strudel filled with poppy seeds and walnuts.

Thinking back, emotionally I was more attached to my grandmother than to my father and mother. She lived through a revolution and huge chaos. She lost her husband and lived alone for fifty years. She raised her two children — my mom and her brother — with little money and in constant fear. She was strong and never complained. She was always patient with me. My mom did not have much time to visit her, but I regularly visited her with my huge black Newfoundland dog when I was older.

Although I did not show my appreciation while she was alive, I loved her very much. Sometimes we just don't appreciate people who are around us and helping us every day. We take them for granted. We only feel how much we loved them and miss them when they are gone. That is what happened with my grandma when I realized many years later how significant she was in my life. I know she is very proud of me now when she is reading my book on the Other Side.

I loved my primary school, my classmates and my teachers. I was one of the top students, and I always got the best marks. The teachers liked me very much: I was appreciated and noticed, so I felt loved. I often performed in front of an audience as the main character in the school play.

School excursions were always fun. Every year we went to a forest where we played an outdoor strategic game between two teams. Everybody got a piece of paper with a five-digit number they stuck to their forehead. The object was to hide so nobody could see your number, except you weren't allowed to hide your number with your hand. When someone said your number out loud, you were out. This game could last for hours because there were plenty of hiding places in a forest. I still remember the mix of fear and excitement I felt when I played.

In Grade 8 we all dressed up as famous singers and performed a show. I wore high-heeled shoes and a mini skirt. My hair was curled, and I wore gorgeous make up. I felt attractive and beautiful, and the show was a huge success. We regularly went to the lake to skate. Occasionally we had a "skating party" with music. I loved these parties on the ice as everyone from the village was there: guys played hockey and girls did figure skating.

It was eight wonderful years before my parents sent me to a boarding school at the age of fourteen. They said I could get a better-quality education because of the strong language program there, which was true. The high school they sent me to was one of the most reputable ones in the country. I know they wanted the best for me. What they did not understand is that a fourteen-year-old is still a child and needs her mother and family support. The teenage years are the most challenging ones. One wants to be independent but still needs guidance and emotional support.

At boarding school, I shared a room with seven girls. There were four metal-framed bunk beds with uncomfortable mattresses for eight girls. The room was so small that nothing could fit beside the bed. The teachers always turned off the lights at 10:00 p.m. so I could not study anymore. I hated it there. After six months my parents decided to take me out of the dormitory, but they kept me in the same school.

I moved into an apartment with my brother where I could study late. My day started at 8:30 a.m. and I usually got home around 6:00 p.m. After a full day of school, I always had private lessons, which I disliked. I studied until midnight every day. I was exhausted, I had no free time, no family, and I felt alone and unloved. I could do whatever I wanted to do — my parents weren't around — but all I did was study day and night. My grandmother often visited and cooked for us.

I remember a school trip when we went canoeing. It was a big class with over thirty students and two male teachers. Most of us had no experience canoeing, so it was not easy paddling and keeping the canoe balanced. We started on a river, which connected to a deep and vast lake. When we reached the lake, some of my classmates started to panic and wanted to return because they felt unsafe. So, the class was split into two. Half the class continued into the lake while the other half planned to return the same way back on the river. I was sitting with two or three girls in the canoe and one of them dropped her paddle into a whirlpool of the river and it disappeared. It was scary. That is my last memory. I don't remember how we made it back. Every time I think about this trip, I have an unsettling, bad feeling.

During the four years of high school, most of the time I went home for the weekends, which I loved. I had delicious homemade meals and slept in long and late in my own comfy bed. Some of my best memories are the weekends I spent with my best friend at her house. We had lots of fun together and often went out to dance. I also went skiing with friends a few times, usually staying for a week. I felt free and joyous during these exciting trips. Even though I have some great memories, I mostly felt alone and exhausted from studying. Many years later I wondered why my parents sent me away to a different city. I did not want to go to that city and that high school, nor did I want to be separated from my family. But nobody asked me.

I argued a lot with my father during these years. As a teenager I also cried a lot in my room. I felt lonely and sad. My mom always listened to my problems, but she would not give me any advice. We never talked about sex. We did not talk much about jobs, careers or goals either, so essentially, I was just going with the flow unconsciously.

My anger toward my parents grew over the years. I was furious with my father when I realized how he mistreated and ignored us. Many years later I understood the scale of the damage he had done to his family and how much it hurt us emotionally. I was also upset with my mom when I finally noticed her manipulations. For example, when I did something "wrong" as a child or I did not listen to her as a teenager she would say, "I will tell your father." In a way, she used my fear of my father to discipline me. For years I blamed my parents unconsciously for many failures in my life.

Laura as a child

Chapter Two

College and University

One of the most remarkable memories I have from college was from when I was about nineteen years old. After spending some time in the sauna, I went back to the pool to talk to my swimming coach. While talking to him, I fainted and fell to the ground unconscious. My coach tried to catch me, but he couldn't. I hit my head extremely hard on the tiled pool deck. While I was unconscious, I had a short visit to the Other Side. Everything was stunning. I can't even describe what I saw and felt — it cannot be compared to anything on Earth. I saw lots of lights, golden and green colours. It was the most wonderful and peaceful feeling I had ever experienced. It was such a disappointment to come back after regaining consciousness. I looked around and saw the pool and my teacher lifting up my legs and trying to wake me up.

"How is your head? Does it hurt? How is your head?" He kept asking.

"I'm OK," I said. "I have no pain in my head."

I just don't want to be here, I thought. I want to
go back so much.

I have wonderful memories from my three years at college. I
enjoyed listening to the professors' interesting presentations and
lectures. It was a boarding school but this one was different from
my high school. We had a very pleasant, spacious room and I only
had one roommate. My roommate became my best friend and we
usually talked late into the night. Twice a year we had a stressful
and busy six-week period when we had exams. Most of the time
I easily passed my exams. We had huge parties where lots of
students from different universities would meet, dance and party.
Sometimes we had two, three parties a week, so I was often tired
the next day during class.

After graduating from college, I continued my higher education at
a university. My roommate also applied, and we were both accepted
for a two-year program. Once again, we became roommates and
classmates for another two years. We continued our free fun life
with partying and studying.

I was not very conscious or wise about my relationships during
college and university partly because I never had a good male role
model. I was missing a positive daughter-father relationship. This
relationship — whether positive or negative — has a huge impact
on a girl's life and her future intimate relationships. The only
relationship I had with my father was negative and destructive, full
of anger, fear, disappointment, arguments, and sadness. Thinking
back, it is not all that surprising that I never had an emotionally
intimate and fulfilling relationship.

I had my first long-term relationship — about a year — during
college. He was handsome with big, blue eyes and blonde hair. He
was very wild which was attractive to me. I was in "blind love."

Why do I call it blind? I could not think clearly, and I was very emotional. I didn't really know him and he didn't know me either. He had a fast motorcycle. We often went to the mountains where the roads are extremely sinuous and dangerous, so he had to tilt the motorcycle very low in the tight turns, which was thrilling. At times he would speed up on highways and pass cars extremely fast. It was exhilarating. He ended our relationship abruptly, and I don't know the reason why to this day. I was absolutely devastated and heartbroken.

During university I had two long-term and a few short-term relationships. I also started to explore relationships with girls, so I went out to clubs where I could meet them. My first boyfriend at university was very handsome. He loved dancing so we went out a lot. He never had money, so I always had to pay for drinks and food. He loved watching soccer. One time I was cutting the grass in my mother's garden, and he was watching a soccer game. He didn't offer any help. He was very easy-going, lazy and laid-back. He did not care much about anything except for his comfort and having fun.

After breaking up with him I dated an extremely intelligent guy (that's what I liked about him). After graduation we decided to go to the USA for a summer job in Yellowstone National Park. I had never travelled that far before, so it sounded like a big adventure. We also thought that we would save some money. Moreover, we wanted to improve our language skills. I hardly spoke English at that time, so overall it sounded like a great idea.

When we arrived in Yellowstone it felt like we were at the end of the world. I had never left Europe, so this was a big deal for me. I was out of my comfort zone, and the park was rather isolated. The surroundings were beautiful: lots of wild animals and wonders of nature. We saw the famous geyser, Old Faithful, that shoots water into the air every day. This summer job program was well organized. They provided us with everything: accommodation, meals three times a day and a uniform. On my first day of work I fainted in the kitchen from the hot steam coming from the giant dishwashers, so the manager decided to find me another job. I started to clean hotel rooms — which was better than the hot kitchen, but not for me.

I was so proud when I got my first cheque in US dollars. We had planned to stay for three months, but I only stayed for five weeks. I decided to return alone to Europe and my boyfriend stayed (we broke up soon after his return). Even returning was difficult. I left the park Friday morning and got home by Sunday evening. I was on a bus for an entire day and spent a night at the airport in San Francisco. I didn't sleep for two nights and I hardly ate anything. I was very nervous during the whole trip. I did not speak English very well, and I felt vulnerable travelling alone. I was exhausted and hungry when I arrived home. This adventure didn't turn out as I expected. I did not appreciate the beauty and power of nature like I do today. I'm sure if I were go back now, it would be a completely different and wonderful experience.

During college and university, I regularly went home for the weekends just like in high school and spent time with my family and friends. I continued revolting against my father's verbal aggression, and I fought him a lot. I tried to protect my mother and my brother from his rage, but we just ended up screaming. I thought I could shield them from his anger, but I could not. He often intimidated my mom and me when we tried to resist him.

All I wanted from my dad was *a few kind words, attention and love.* He never gave me that. I also yearned for his approval. What I wanted the most was for him to be *proud of me.* Many children — later adults — feel similarly. We want validation from our parents and later from our spouses, managers and friends. Young adults often choose a profession that their parents suggest or inherit a family business. Ten, fifteen or twenty years later they realize they are not happy in their career and wonder why they made that choice. It's because they wanted their parents' approval.

Sometimes I wish I could go back to college with the knowledge and wisdom I have right now. What would I do differently? What kind of life would I choose to live? I know there is no point thinking about the past because I did the best I could and in the way I wanted. By the end of my book you will understand what I mean.

Chapter Three

My Marriage

Ihave always been a compassionate, kind, empathetic and open-minded woman. However, at twenty-four years old I had very low self-esteem, little confidence, and I lacked self-love and self-worth. I had no idea I was missing these and how important self-care and my well-being was. On the other hand, I had high expectations for myself. I wanted to be perfect and meet what I thought were other people's expectations. I was unconsciously searching for what I missed as a child. I needed acceptance and attention but mostly love and kindness. Now I know it is crucial to accept and love ourselves. Once we love ourselves, accept who we are and believe we are worthy, we receive the love, attention and appreciation we have been looking for.

After returning from the USA I started to look for a job, which is when I met Sofia. Beautiful, thin and tall with brown hair and brown eyes, she was kind and affectionate. We enjoyed each other's company and she treated me with love.

She also helped me secure my first full-time job in an office. Part of my job was interpretation between various members of the company I worked for. In May 2002, I was invited to a three-day international conference in a famous wine region of Europe to facilitate conversations with important clients. The dry business during the day didn't dull the beautiful countryside I found myself in. The fresh air and fragrant mists off the expansive lake that bordered the hotel were intoxicating. At the end of each day, the company hosted elegant dinner parties with fine local food and drink. I met my husband, let's call him Paul, on a dinner cruise on that still, beautiful lake. As I gazed across the dance floor, like a moment in a Hollywood movie his greyish blue eyes caught my bright blue eyes and I was hooked. As he approached, I knew we would make a striking pair. Handsome, dashing and, as I soon found out, intelligent and kind, he seemed to be everything I was looking for.

We spent more and more time together and I discovered he was so different from the boys I dated in college and university. He was the perfect gentleman, charming to a fault, confident and thoughtful. He had a fantastic, high-paying job at an international organization and a degree from one of the most reputable universities in Canada. He was calm and patient. He was funny and generous. The first bouquet I received from him was a stunning arrangement of countless red roses.

I felt lucky and special.

When I met Paul, I was in a relationship with Sofia. He asked me to break up with her, so I did. Sofia was furious with him even though she had only met him once. I think she knew intuitively, deep down, that he was not good for me. As our relationship progressed, Paul said he was not comfortable with me dating women, so I promised not to. For years, I was not with any women even though I wanted to be. I didn't realize it, but I had already given up part of who I was. It was difficult, but I did it anyway. I had to deny part of myself to stay with him. Later, I understood that he controlled me from the very beginning although it was not clear and obvious to me at the time.

Perhaps I was blinded by the good life. In the first year of our relationship he bought me a gold watch for my birthday and a beautiful gold bracelet for Christmas. We dated for a year before I moved into his apartment. We were both busy with our interesting, decent-paying jobs and everyday life. We travelled a lot and had many weekend getaways. We often visited a different European city and stayed there for a night or two. We went skiing in the Alps every winter and took beach holidays to Egypt. We went for a romantic cruise on the Nile that included delicious meals and a visit to the pyramids of Giza, the Valley of the Kings, and Luxor's Karnak Temple Complex. On a different trip to Egypt, we stayed in Sharm El Sheikh at a luxury resort and snorkelled in the Red Sea. That was a special experience: so many rich colours and creatures living in the sea one cannot imagine. It is a completely different world above and below the surface.

Everything was perfect. Maybe a little too perfect. My fairy tale ended quickly. My romantic, "perfect" relationship turned into a nightmare.

I moved to Canada with Paul in January 2005 after being in relationship with him for three years in my home country. I thought I knew him. I felt three years was long enough to get to know someone and start a family. My intuition told me there was something a bit unusual that made me uneasy. Something was off and I ignored a few signs, like he didn't like kissing. However, my focus was on becoming a mother. My biological clock was ticking. It was an instinctive, natural, strong feeling that overruled any warning signs. Nothing else mattered to me. I thought he would be a good father who could support my children and me. Financial stability, security and having children were my top priorities when we got married in the summer of 2005. I was twenty-seven.

Things started to change quickly after my move to Canada and after our marriage. I was alone in a country I didn't know. Everything was different from the place I grew up: language, culture, people. I did not speak English very well, so I was dependent on Paul every time I had to run an errand or talk to someone. I enrolled in an English language course to improve my language skills, which helped a lot. Living with his mom in the same house was also difficult. I had no friends or family there beyond Paul.

After living in Canada for six months, Paul got a high-paying job at an international organization in Asia, so we moved there in the summer of 2005. I stayed home while he was at work. I studied international relations and earned a bachelor's degree three years later. The country, culture and people were completely different from Europe and Canada and adjusting proved challenging. The city we lived in was polluted, overcrowded, hot and congested. Expatriates can't drive in the city because it is so chaotic, so we had two choices: rent a car with a driver or take taxis everywhere. So, I took taxis everywhere. Due to the poor air quality, I couldn't enjoy my daily walks nor could I do any outdoor activities. Most of the time I had to stay indoors because of the extreme heat and pollution. My freedom of movement was greatly restricted. My new life was rather intolerable, and I was often bored. My days were the same at home: alone, studying for my exams. I had no job, no friends, no family. I became *isolated, unhappy and lonely.*

Paul had a great job with lots of responsibilities and some social life. Sometimes we would meet his colleagues or friends for dinner. But usually after work he was exhausted and needed time alone to relax and recharge while I was full of energy and needed company after a long day alone. When I talked to him, he showed little or no interest. Often, he would not answer my questions or even look at me. I was frustrated and felt unnoticed.

My only company most days was our maid. She cooked every day, shopped for groceries and cleaned the house. Sometimes I would go with her to the market when I needed a break from my studying and from being "locked" in the house. She was always smiling and never complained. She looked happy while I knew she had a hard life. She had two sons to raise, and her husband was disabled. She worked alone for the whole family. She is another person I did not appreciate while she was there for me. I'm so grateful for her help, support and company.

A lot of travelling punctuated the boredom, so I was fortunate in that regard. We went to Bangkok a few times and travelled Thailand to see the Golden Temples, huge Buddha statues, night markets, beautiful beaches and eat the delicious food. It is one of the most fascinating places I ever been. I took every chance I could to get away and travel to Europe to visit my family and friends. I missed fun, joy, laughter and happiness. Life with Paul was missing those elements. Most of the time, it was draining being around him.

That's when I met Steve. He was very handsome with beautiful blue eyes and brown hair. He had the perfect body: tall, athletic, strong and muscular. At first it was romantic, and we did not have an intimate relationship for a long time. I received everything from him I did not from Paul. Steve paid attention to me and listened to what I had to say. We spent lots of time together swimming, running and dancing. We had great conversations and we laughed a lot. After many platonic dates, we finally kissed. It was the most romantic and passionate kiss I have ever experienced. Paul never liked kissing. He only liked sex.

Steve was like a magnet. I felt such a strong physical attraction toward him that I could not resist. It is difficult to describe; one must feel it. After the first kiss I never wanted to stop kissing him. I resisted having sex with Steve for a long time because I did not want to cheat on Paul — my mind wouldn't let me. I knew what I was doing was wrong. When we finally had sex, I could not enjoy it because I could not relax. I felt incredibly stressed. The truth was we hadn't spent enough time getting to know each other well. All I knew was that I felt wonderful and joyous when I was with him.

What was his secret? Besides being incredibly handsome, he knew the "language of women." He knew what a woman wants and needs. He made me believe he cared about me and that I was beautiful and worthy. Most men don't understand women. (Maybe most women don't understand men either). Most men don't know that a woman does *everything* for a man and later for her children if she feels *loved, respected and appreciated.* By contrast, if a woman is humiliated, ignored and disrespected — or worse, psychologically and emotionally abused for years — she will resist and revolt sooner or later.

Mutual respect and *equal treatment of women* is key not only within families but at a societal and global level. Physical attraction is important in a relationship; however, a man should see significantly more in a woman than her sexy, attractive body, a housewife, a great cook or the mother of his children. It is hard for some men to see women as spiritual beings and see beyond their bodies and physical appearances. It is crucial that women and men treat each other with respect and see themselves as equal partners. This is the only way we will understand each other and have harmonious relationships.

Everything would have been different if I knew then what I know now. I remember sitting on an airplane and writing a letter that expressed my feelings for Steve. All I knew was that I felt great when I was with him — I was joyous, free, happy, smiling and laughing all the time. I actually wanted to get off the plane and end my relationship with Paul. My heart told me to get off the plane and my mind told me to stay. I listened to my mind. I was sick during the whole flight because my body disagreed with my decision. My inner struggle manifested itself as a severe stomach-ache. It was tearing me apart inside out. Returning to Paul and giving up my fun relationship with Steve was against my heart and my soul. My body and heart tried to tell me that, but I would not listen.

Why didn't I leave Paul? I was too weak and scared to follow my heart. My mind and my ego were too controlling. So, I returned to the "known." I decided to tell Paul about my affair because the guilt was so overwhelming that I could not keep this secret inside me. He was furious and outraged. I believe from that point on he lived in suppressed anger and resentment toward me. He did not forgive me for years and confronted me every time he had a chance.

Chapter Four

The Birth of My Children: Amazing Women and Mothers

After two years in Asia, we moved back to Canada in 2007. I landed my first job at a local non-governmental organization. Later I worked for two other organizations while I tried to get pregnant unsuccessfully for almost two years. The doctors found out by chance during a blood test that I had serious thyroid hormone imbalances. Once my thyroid level was restored to a normal level, I got pregnant instantly.

Our first child, Mia, was born in Canada in 2009. After Mia's birth, Paul started to criticize me all the time. He always had to be right about everything. Nothing I did was good enough. As a mother I knew intuitively what to do with my baby, but he did not like any of that. We argued a lot, often in front our little daughter. It was exhausting to always have to prove myself and defend my decisions. Our relationship had entered a destructive cycle, and I cried a lot during that time. After our daughter's birth I was even more dependent on him than before, which he knew. I once burst out crying and told him, "*I will leave you one day!*" He looked up from the computer and arrogantly told me, "Good luck!"

I stayed home with Mia for a year before I went back to work to begin an exhausting cycle that every working mom knows. I worked in an office, did household labour and looked after our child. I shopped for groceries, cooked and cleaned and did not get a kind word or much help from Paul. Most of the time he stared at his computer or watched television when I talked to him. Often, he did not respond when I asked a question. I was *unnoticed, ignored and unappreciated* for years.

We lived our automated lives unconsciously and unaware. (Later I realized as long as we are unconscious, we don't know that we are unconscious therefore we can't make different choices in our lives.) Every day was the same monotonous and repetitive circle. Darting to work, rushing to pick up hungry Mia from day care, making dinner, cleaning up, putting Mia to bed and then collapsing into sleep in order to start over the next day. We had some friends from work, but I did not have any close friends I could talk to about my difficulties. Sometimes I talked to my cousin who also lived in Canada, but of course she was busy with her own life and two children.

Paul started to drink. Not much — two glasses of red wine a day — but it was enough for him to be "numb" every evening. Alcohol offered him a short time of happiness and temporary relief from his suffering. It was a switch off for him. While drinking, he turned off his mind and sat at his computer looking distressed and miserable.

While meeting everybody's expectations and pleasing others, I neglected my body and ignored important messages my heart and soul sent me. I wasn't able to interpret these messages, and I dismissed my intuitions. I had a compulsion — a strong urge — to meet everybody's expectations and prove myself worthy. Working in an office and earning money was one way to show my worthiness. I wanted to be accepted and valued.

> I wanted to be the *perfect mother*, so I did everything for my daughter.

> I wanted to be the *perfect wife*, so I did everything for my husband.

> I wanted to be the *perfect housewife*, so I did all the household labour even though I was exhausted.

Many women do the same every day. They manage two or three full-time jobs: their regular job, childcare and household labour. I thought if I can "do it all" I would be appreciated, loved and respected. That was not the case. We don't have to be the perfect mother, attractive wife, flawless housewife, ideal co-worker or successful businesswoman simultaneously. It is impossible to meet all these expectations and play these many roles at the same time. We can have it all, but maybe not all at the same time. I found that as I reached for it all, I paid a heavy price.

In the last fifty years a lot has changed in terms of gender equality. Having said that, women continue to sacrifice their careers after the birth of their children more often than men. Making up for the years women spend at home with their children — anywhere from a few months to several years — is not easy when re-entering the job market. The wage gap is still significant between women and men. In addition, women usually spend more time on unpaid household labour than men. This all adds up to so many women having little to no time and energy for self-care (I always put my kids first, then my husband. I was the last person in the family I would care for).

Society expects women to "do it all", which is a very high standard. You can do it all, but you don't have to. It is your choice! It's OK to stay home with your baby for one, two or more years — as long you want — without having another job. It's also OK to go back to work and find a suitable day care for your children. It is all good. I always became a bit annoyed when someone asked me, "What do you do for work?" and I'd answer, "I'm home with my baby" or "I'm a stay-at-home mom." The conversation suddenly stopped. Raising children is not a "real job" in many people's eyes.

Being a stay-at-home mom is one of the most rewarding, wonderful, important and difficult jobs in the Universe. Sometimes I, like many women, felt less valued and judged. It is OK. Do what you think is the best for yourself and your children. Don't let others decide for you. We are not less valuable just because we don't have a career with promotions and a high salary. You and I raise the next generation that will shape our world and impact our future. That is how important our job is! No position, no career, no money, no business can match it! So *be proud* of what you are doing and don't seek validation from other people.

Women hold the family together, so it is important to find the right balance between paid and unpaid work, time with our families and time alone. If we feel off balance, which is often the case after the birth of a baby, it is important to make changes in our lives and ask for help to rebalance. If we are happy and balanced, everyone in the family is happy and balanced. If we feel overwhelmed, overworked and stressed, it will be reflected in the family. Taking good care of ourselves is just as important as taking care of others.

When I was pregnant with our second child, Lyon, I left my office job a few months before my delivery date and took Mia out of day care because she was very unhappy there. It turned out to be a great decision because I really enjoyed that year. We took daily walks in the park pushing the big red stroller with Mia in it while my belly was huge with Lyon. We often went to a playground and story time at the library. Those are precious memories when I felt perfect peace. I was calm and patient all the time. Nobody could upset me during those months. Lyon was born in 2012. Mia stayed home with us for a year after.

When Mia was three and Lyon a few months old, I broke my elbow while skating. I could not lift a plate, change a diaper or do anything with my hand. I was in pain and felt awful that I couldn't look after my baby, but I did not expect Paul's odd reaction. He was angry with me for not being able to look after our children. He was frozen and blocked, which meant he could not look after the kids nor assist me. I have a vivid memory of Paul slumped over the kitchen counter looking stressed and annoyed. I knew that something was not right, but I could not explain his unusual behaviour. He showed zero empathy or compassion toward me. My mother had to fly from Europe to help us until I recovered. This "accident" was one of the first strong signals I received to change my life, but I ignored it. I felt stuck. I had two young children, and I was completely dependent on Paul.

My automated life during that time meant I had no time for myself. We did not go out much; if we did, an argument ruined the night. In those running, busy, overloaded years I hardly noticed how unhappy and lonely I was. I was too distracted to see what was going on in my life. I did not slow down or think much about it.

Many people do the same. We keep ourselves busy, so we don't have to face our real problems (i.e., being "lost," alone, unhappy, isolated, etc.). Most people are not comfortable being alone and looking within. Media, movies, negative news, TV shows and social media successfully distract people's attention from the real problems.

I invite you to spend some time with yourself and connect with your spirit, your higher self. It is important to get to know yourself — your true self: who you really are and what you want. Listen to your intuition and gut feelings. As part of my awakening a few years later, I spent a lot of time thinking about and writing down my short- and long-term goals, which kept me focused on what I wanted to achieve. Additionally, I created a list about "How to live (and die) without regrets." These two exercises were helpful in evaluating my life, goals and desires. When I look back at my notes, diary and positive affirmations over the last five years, it is amazing and almost unbelievable how far I have come and how many goals I have achieved.

Positive thinking and attitude are the first steps to achieving your goals. This is followed by planning and taking actions.

1. Create two separate lists:
    One with your goals (short-term: one year; and long-term: five to ten years) and another with things you want to do before you die (there might be some overlaps, and that is OK). Write down everything that is important to you. It does not matter whether you believe it possible or you doubt you can achieve this goal — just keep writing until you have no more to write. Goals can be small: make more friends, kiss someone, laugh often, dance with someone or learn something new. Or they can be big: buy a new car, land a dream job, vacation in the Caribbean, find inner peace and forgiveness. Try to include a few items that are not materialistic but are helpful for your heart and

soul (i.e., do something for your community, the planet or nature). You don't need grand goals. Sometimes small successes will bring more happiness and fulfillment than huge accomplishments.

2. Plan what you can do to achieve these goals.
   Beliefs and thoughts are powerful. The more you believe you can achieve something the more likely it is you will succeed. Repeating positive affirmations can bring many wonderful changes in your life. Don't think about what you do not want. *Think about what you do want.* For example:

   > "I'm in a wonderful relationship with a kind, loving person."

   > "I have a fulfilling, meaningful job with thoughtful co-workers and I earn good money."

   > "I'm loved and appreciated."

3. Take action.
   Once you have a goal and you take action, the Universe will support you to meet your goal. You will be surprised how many items on your list will be fulfilled when you look back a few years later. It is important to have faith in yourself and in the Universe. You don't have to know everything; you have to believe it! Trust the Universe that everything will work out magnificently for you.

The following *questions* can help you with your list of goals:

- Do you know what makes you happy and laugh?
- Do you love your job?

- Are you truly happy in your relationship/marriage?
- Do you have an ideal work/life balance?
- Do you have time for yourself and things you enjoy?
- Are you grateful for all you have?
- Do you spend quality time with your children?
- Do you have clear goals?
- Do you have friends and a social network that can support you when you need it?
- How much time do you spend outdoors in nature?
- Do you sleep enough?
- Are you eating nourishing food?
- Do you live in fear?
- Is your life full of stress?
- How many hours a day do you use the computer and/or watch TV?
- Do you listen to your intuition and inner voice?
- Do you enjoy the present, or do you live in the past or the future?
- What are you passionate about?
- How can you help other people or animals?

Later, you can ask deeper questions:

- Why are you here?
- Where do you go when you "die"?
- Why did you create this life?
- Can you change your reality and recreate your life?
- Can you have a life you always wanted and dreamt of?
- What is holding you back?
- What is your purpose?
- What kind of life lessons did you have so far and what have you learnt from these experiences?
- What is the meaning of your life?

Chapter Five

Living Abroad: The Deterioration of My Marriage

When Lyon was just over one year old, Paul got a job in Western Europe, so we were on the move again in January 2014. After living in Canada for seven years I was excited to be going back to Europe again. I would be close to my home country, so I could fly home easily and visit my family frequently.

I was constantly planning for my future happiness and it never came. We knew in advance that we would move, so I lived in the future while organizing the sale of our house and packing up in Canada. I imagined our perfect, happy life in Europe while I hardly noticed my present in Canada. I wasted precious time in the now while hoping that this move, new environment, new country would change things and improve my relationship with Paul.

We had everything we could wish for: a beautiful, spacious house with an enormous garden, a luxury car and an international private school for our children. We went on beach holidays and skied in the picturesque Alps. We had a comfortable life. Paul had a demanding job he liked. I recreated the same life and reality in Western Europe that I had in Canada: a good salary and an office job I did not like, in an unpleasant work environment.

I was busy organizing everything — my job, the household and two children — without much support from Paul. I was driving around a lot with the kids to doctors, school and their activities. Sometimes Paul was helpful, but most of the time I had to manage everything on my own. At one point, Lyon got very sick. I was trying to contact our doctor but could not reach her. Every time I dialed the number it went to voicemail. I was stressed and often anxious when one of my children got sick or had a high fever. I called Paul and asked for his help, but instead of getting his son to the doctor, he said he was busy with work and couldn't do anything. I was on my own. I was outraged.

Most people think if they move to a bigger house, a different country, save more money, change jobs, start a business, get married, buy another car, go on vacation, buy more clothes, etc. they will be happy. I was no different. I fantasized that moving to a new country, living in a big house and taking fancy vacations — all these materialistic things — could make me happy. I was wrong. Believe me.

I felt *a big emptiness inside*. I was so unhappy.

Our consumer society with its marketing campaigns convinces us to accumulate things we don't need and makes us believe products bring happiness. We are led to believe that once we "have it all" we will be whole and happy. But we still feel the same: unhappy, dissatisfied and empty inside. Some people look for their happiness in drugs, smoking, partying, drinking, having sex and eating excessively.

I remember being at a club alone and striking up a conversation with a kind couple. They seemed happy together.

"What would you like to drink?" the man asked me.

I told him I don't drink alcohol when I drive.

"Do you smoke?" he asked.

I don't smoke.

"Drugs?"

Nope.

He was shocked and said, "You don't drink, smoke or do drugs. What do you do then?"

No amount of money, drugs, food, alcohol or sex can eliminate our unhappiness or emptiness. We can't buy, eat or drink our problems away. It is difficult to get out of the vicious cycle of "craving, needing and wanting" because it never ends. We always hope we've found what we have been looking for, and we'll finally feel complete, joyful and loved. Then we are disappointed, and the search starts again. As long as we believe all of those materialistic and mind-altering substances can give us happiness, we will be desperately searching. By the end of the book you will understand how and why I stopped my "search."

My marriage was *in ruins*. It did not matter what I did; our relationship continued downhill. Some days Paul was kind and we could have a normal conversation. Most of the time, he was exhausted and distressed. He was unable to show affection and emotional intimacy. All he wanted was physical intercourse. Sometimes I refused to have sex with him, which made him even angrier. It got so bad that even though I did not feel like having sex with him, I occasionally agreed so he would remain calm and kind. Increasingly, it felt like an obligation to have sex with him.

I was often impatient, irritable and frustrated with my children and with Paul. I experienced tremendous mood swings. I frequently had angry outbursts. While we had everything in a materialistic way, we had nothing in a spiritual and emotional way. I was disconnected from my higher self and from God/Goddess.

All I ever wanted from Paul was attention, love and kindness. I'm a very compassionate, empathic person, so his personality was in strong contrast with my nature. Paul showed no kindness and he was ignorant most of the time. He was arrogant when I had a different opinion and resisted him. He had a controlling personality and influenced me for his own self-interest (which I did not notice at the time). He often dismissed my view and belittled my ideas. He never treated me as his equal partner.

He always has been a master at twisting things around. Over the years I tried many times to have a conversation with him about his behaviour and how I felt in our marriage, but he would not take any responsibility for his own behaviour and deflected everything back to me. During arguments he always made me believe that I was the problem and that something was wrong with me — and I believed him (though today I know I wasn't the problem). He manipulated me at such a high level that it was difficult to see what he was actually doing. I didn't. I found out later that he was lying to me all along. I did not see that either because he covered it up so professionally.

Paul was a different person in public and at work. He was funny, polite, and kind at office parties and receptions when he put on his "public face and image." His appearance meant a lot to him.

He bought expensive suits and coats while I was trying to save money. We had many arguments over the years about his luxury shopping and excessive spending. Everything had to look perfect and expensive on him, which matched his ambition and success. He worked hard on his career and the prestige it came with. He looked flawless to the outside world and acted completely differently in public and in private.

I know I'm not alone and there are women struggling in similar relationships. I know how you feel. I have been there. Women are frequently in denial or they think their partner's behaviour is "normal." They often blame themselves for their deteriorating marriage. Sometimes they rationalize their husband's behaviour and soothe themselves by thinking it is OK, not so bad or could be worse. Thoughts such as, "Other women have worse marriages" and "Every relationship has its challenges so it wouldn't be different with another man" are common while clinging to the hope that he will get better and life will improve. Thoughts like these keep these women trapped in an unhappy marriage. They silently suffer for the sake of their children. They do their best to keep the family and their dysfunctional marriages together at the expense of their own emotional, mental and physical health and their happiness.

I did not know how important it is to pay attention to good and bad energy around us. I was trying to live my life by shutting Paul out as much as I could. However, every time I felt joyous, he made a tremendous effort to drag me down and drain my energy. No matter how much I tried to isolate myself from him, he was still around because we lived in the same house. You probably know what I'm talking about. There are people who energize us and we like being around. When we are surrounded by "good vibes" we feel happy and energized. There are also people who drain us and make us feel exhausted. Paul was one of them. When we are surrounded by "bad vibes" our energy decreases and our health declines. That is what happened to me while I was being sucked into Paul's downward spiral.

In my marriage:

> **I was invisible, unloved and unnoticed.**

> **I felt helpless, hopeless and trapped.**

> **I was emotionally and physically exhausted.**

> **I felt powerless.**

> **My energy was being drained when I was around Paul.**

> **My soul was drowning. Literally.**

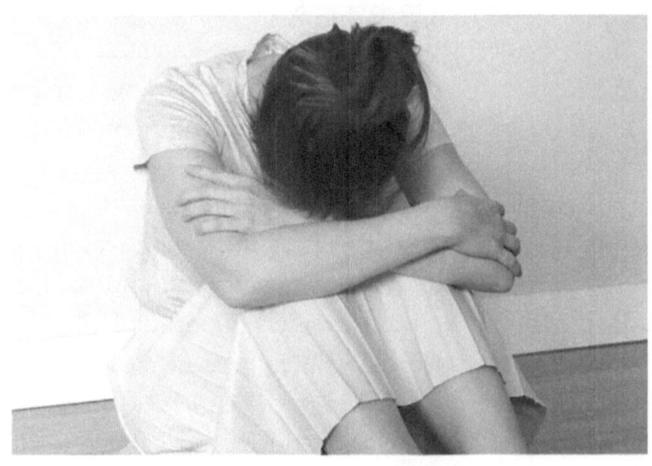

Chapter Six

Trying to Save
My Marriage

While our marriage was going downhill, I was committed to saving it for the sake of our children. We decided to spice things up and go to adult clubs. We both wanted to try something new, and I was desperately trying to fill the growing void between us and in myself.

One of the reasons we started to go to adult clubs was to receive what we didn't in our marriage. It is the wrong reason though. One of my unfulfilled desires was kissing. Paul did not like it so we hardly kissed, but sex was extremely important for him. These clubs were perfect for bisexual women because most women who hung out there were attracted to both genders, as I am. Finally, some of my desires were being fulfilled, and I found a friendly, open-minded atmosphere in these clubs.

Most people go to these clubs to live out their desires and fantasies and have sex with other people without cheating on each other.

Some want to reignite their monotonous, dull and boring sex life. They go as a couple, find another couple or a single woman (extremely rare) and play. Everyone agrees to the rules of the game: no lies and no cheating. I find this is better than infidelity and deception in a relationship. Some of these couples looked happy, strongly connected and sexually fulfilled. We were not one of those couples. We were unhappy and sexually unfulfilled. I know it must seem like a strange decision, but it was just an experience like everything else in life. We choose our experiences and make decisions — "right" or "wrong" — about everything in our lives.

We visited many different and exciting clubs in Europe and North America, but we never met a couple we both liked and who liked us. Finding mutual sympathy and attraction among four people is challenging. I was not attracted to men in these clubs, so I focused on having fun with women and had no problem meeting beautiful women who were also attracted to me. I really enjoyed it, especially in New York City.

Paul often ruined the night as we repeatedly argued in the car driving home from the club. He would get frustrated and angry with me. He blamed me because the night did not go as he planned. I felt terrible. After a while I did not feel like going out with him anymore, so we went out less every year. Eventually I stopped going out with him all together.

At one point I even suggested we try an open marriage, which he refused. You will understand later why. Today I know an open marriage would not have been the solution nor solved our problems, but I couldn't see it then.

For years I tried to convince Paul to get professional help and attend couple's therapy to save our marriage. He always refused except for the time I threatened a divorce. We had a few sessions, but this last-minute counselling made no significant difference. It was too little, too late. Every time he refused couple's therapy, I felt stuck and helpless. I went to counselling alone, but it was not enough.

At one point I was very desperate and seriously considered leaving him, but I was not able to start an independent life. When I first tried to divorce him, we separated but lived in one house for a few months. Paul's employer paid for the house we rented and for the children's international school, so I could not move anywhere. I was stuck. I was not yet strong enough emotionally, physically, or financially to leave him. I was full of fear. I did not have a steady job or income. I had no support network, friends or family. I had two small children and responsibilities I could not dismiss. I was completely dependent on Paul, and he knew it.

He had *all the power*. I was *powerless*.

It was not the right time for a divorce. Now I know there is never a "right time" — it is good to do it before your marriage consumes you and crushes your soul. Here is the tricky part though: as long you live in fear and ask questions like, "How can I raise my children alone?" "Do I get a job?" "Where will I live?" "Will I have enough money for everything?" "Who will look after the children if I get sick?" it seems overwhelming. When you overcome your fears, change becomes easier. Planning is great; however, you don't have to know every detail.

If you feel controlled, powerless, scared, unloved and emotionally exhausted in your relationship or in your marriage, the best you can do for yourself is listen to your heart, your soul and your inner voice. Trust your instincts! They will guide you in the right direction. Listen to your feelings. Connect to your inner wisdom and feminine power.

Do you feel great around him or drained all the time? Do you feel loved, respected and appreciated? Do you feel invisible, helpless and trapped? These are simple questions that can help you decide.

If women knew how much inner power and wisdom they posses deep inside, it would be easier to take back control of their lives. You can choose to stay in the relationship, or you can choose to leave. I'm not here to tell you what to do. You are the only one who can decide in your own life. You create your own experiences. Don't let anybody control you or decide for you. You can always ask for help and listen to others' opinions. At the end of the day *only you know what serves you the best.*

Today I know some relationships and marriages *cannot be saved or they are not worth saving.* It is not worthwhile to give up who you are while trying to meet your partner's expectations. Slowly, piece by piece, I was losing myself in my marriage while I tried everything — more than a woman in a traditional or conventional relationship would be comfortable with — to fix it.

It was *not enough.*

I know now what I did not realize for years: if a relationship is broken and miserable for many years, it is best to find a solution *sooner* rather than later. Your emotional health and well-being have a significant impact on your physical health. They are strongly connected, and you will soon understand what I mean.

Eckhart Tolle wrote a great summary in *The Power of Now* (2004) that characterizes my marriage with Paul perfectly. It says that couples compromise to stay in a broken relationship because they are afraid of staying alone or because this is what they get used to. Others decide to remain in a negative relationship for their children or security (p.157).

We compromised and stayed in a dysfunctional relationship for longer than we should have. I stayed for the children and for financial security. Paul stayed for sex, comfort and the kids. We stayed because that is what we learnt from our parents and because society expected us to raise our children in a marriage. My parents celebrated their fiftieth wedding anniversary in December 2019. Fifty years sounds like a long time, but how many years were they genuinely happy during that half century? That is the important question. My guess is not too many.

My opinion about marriages has changed drastically over the years. I don't believe in the institution of marriage anymore. They are often not as fabulous and glamorous as in the movies. The reality can be very different from romantic movies and fairy tales. The façade of joy and happiness often hides unhappy and disappointed people. We post so many happy family photos on social media that are meant to demonstrate how fortunate we are. Really? Or is there something behind those happy, smiling faces? I remember posting those pictures of us — we posed and smiled on the beach or ski vacations. Who would have guessed what was really behind those happy faces?

I have also come to realize that marriage limits a person's sexual freedom and restricts their sexuality. Societal, religious and moral restrictions are forced upon us in marriage. We are not supposed to have sexual relationships with other people in a marriage. I think most people, by nature, are attracted to many people (certainly more than one), but they don't admit it. Sparks and excitement are long gone, especially after eight to ten years of marriage. Moreover, bisexual people are attracted to both genders. It is normal to be attracted to other people. There is nothing wrong with it.

What is wrong and unhealthy is to suppress desires and attraction and keep suffering just to hold a relationship together. Living in deception, lies and guilt is also unhealthy. What do I mean by that? People stay faithful and suffer in a marriage when they are attracted to someone else. Their mind reminds them that it is wrong to want someone else and often prevents them from fulfilling their desires. They hide their feelings and deny their physical attraction toward the other person. At times they are so powerfully drawn to another person (as has been my case) that it is impossible to resist. If they satisfy their desires, they suffer in lies and guilt. If they stay faithful, they resist their desires. Either way, these people often face conflicting choices, and they suffer whether they act with or against their hearts.

I have done both and suffered greatly in both cases. I lived with the guilt of my affair until I told Paul the truth. On the other hand, while I remained faithful to Paul throughout most of my marriage, I was sexually unfulfilled and resisted my desires. As the saying goes: *what you resist, persists!* It is so true. The more I resisted my sexual desires the stronger they became. It caused me agonizing suffering and tension over the years.

I believe a relationship should be based on mutual respect and attraction, love, support, understanding, kindness, trust and compromise between two people. Many people have relationships like this. I also believe in soulmate relationships, which are different from most relationships. Some people are lucky enough to find their soulmate. They feel a special, deep-rooted and harmonious connection. Maybe they feel they've met him or her before. They feel respected, appreciated, loved and cherished. They smile and laugh. They radiate and shine. They are happy beyond imagination when they're together. They are sexually fulfilled so they do not desire anybody else. It is magical. If you are one of these lucky people, cherish it every day. You never know how long it will last.

I'm not here to tell anyone what to do or to judge anybody. I'm here to tell *my* truth. This is *my* experience and *my* opinion. Everyone has different views and experiences about marriage. Those opinions are also valid, and those experiences are very real for the person involved. There is no "one truth," but many.

It is unfortunate that many people stay and suffer in broken and miserable marriages because they can't divorce out of fear, obligation and for financial or other reasons. Most of the time fear and uncertainty hold us back. In my opinion, when your soul feels trapped, restricted and not free, it is difficult to feel happy and connected to your higher self.

Chapter Seven

My Disease, My Near-Death Experience, and My Mind Shift

As the elevator rose to the sixth floor, I was frightened and anxious. In the waiting room, a few people were wearing hats and scarfs to cover their bald heads, which scared me even more.

Everything started with an extremely sharp pain in my abdomen in the summer of 2015 while we were on holiday in Canada. Paul called an ambulance, and I was taken to the hospital where I had emergency appendix surgery on July 6th. When they started anesthesia, I was somewhere in between awake and asleep, in a state of both consciousness and unconsciousness, when I found myself in a big, interestingly shaped white room with no windows or doors, and my overwhelming feeling was: *Nothing matters.* Not even my children — who are the most precious people in the world to me — mattered in this place. That is my only memory about the appendix surgery. A week later the surgeon, who specialised in oncology, called to say he wanted to see me.

Paul and the children came with me to the hospital. While waiting for the surgeon I had a terrible feeling. I knew something "bad" was going to happen. I stared blankly at the round table while he said he found a neuroendocrine tumour of approximately 2.5 cm on my appendix during surgery. They successfully removed it, but it was sheer coincidence that they saw it in the first place. He said it is a rare type of cancer, not much research about it. The surgeon recommended more blood tests, CT, and a colonoscopy to rule out liver metastases and synchronous tumours. My surgical report[1] said, "Right hemicolectomy with lymphadenectomy should be seriously considered in view of the risk of nodal metastases."

The word *cancer* scared me so much that I could not think clearly. The surgeon patiently explained everything in great detail, and I listened to him, but I could not understand all the medical terminology. I was in a very disturbed and confused state of mind during the whole conversation. Tears were running down my face, and I could not stop crying. I did not know much about cancer except that I should be terrified of it. At the age of thirty-seven *the life I knew was falling apart.* I was overloaded with fear and uncertainty.

Paul looked both blank and confused. I had a feeling he did not even comprehend how serious this was and what this diagnosis meant to our family and our children. I remember looking at my children through my tears — my daughter was six, my son was three — thinking, *Who will raise them?*

---

[1]   Surgical Report dated on July 6th, 2015

A few days later, I bought my first book about cancer, *Anticancer*[2] by David Servan-Schreiber. It was a rational explanation of my predicament, and it made me feel significantly better and more empowered. I discovered I could do a lot for my health. From that point, I never doubted I would be healed. Educating myself was the best thing I could have done in that situation. I didn't feel so powerless and helpless after I gained some basic knowledge about this disease and what I could do about it.

Anticancer and other books[3] on cancer taught me so much about the causes and contributors to cancer. I learned how cancer is formed into a tumour and what I can do to prevent it from spreading to other parts of the body. I read about anticancer and detoxifying foods — special fruit, vegetables and powerful spices — that effectively fight cancer and inflammation in the body. I also familiarised myself with ways to strengthen and support my immune system to fight this disease. Most importantly, I learned about the anticancer mind, the link between body and mind, the importance of letting go of fear and anger, and the significance of a calm mind and emotional well-being. David Servan-Schreiber emphasizes how important it is to deal with negative feelings such as hopelessness and resolve past problems and traumas in the recovery process (*Anticancer*, p. 175).

After reading a few books and thinking about my relationship and my emotional state, I was not all surprised at my diagnosis. For years I felt helpless and desperate in my marriage, and it contributed to my declining health.

---

[2] David Servan-Schreiber, M.D., Ph.D.: Anticancer, A New Way of Life, Collins, HarperCollins Publishers Ltd, 2008

[3] Ian Gawler: You Can Conquer Cancer – A New Way of Living, Penguin Group, 1984
Richard Béliveau, Ph.D., and Denis Gingras, Ph.D.: Foods that Fight Cancer – Preventing Cancer Through Diet, McClelland & Stewart Ltd., 2005

Cancer affects so many people, and most feel helpless and powerless. Understandably, they are full of fear, stress and emotional suffering. I know the feeling. I have been there. I'm no expert but based on my experiences and the information I gathered, there are so many things one can do to fight cancer in addition to the doctors' recommendations and medical treatments. We can start by making meaningful changes in our lives if we are diagnosed with cancer or any chronic disease. It would be even better to start these lifestyle changes before the diagnosis.

I was determined to change my life, get regular exercise, transform my diet, follow doctor's orders and live to raise my children. I started by rebranding the cancer as a "disease." I never liked the word "cancer," and I decided to stop using it. Focusing on my diet and regular exercise was not enough. I had to concentrate on emotional healing and mental health as well. It was important to find techniques that calmed my mind and released tension. When we are calm and balanced our bodies are free to work in the most efficient way to support our immune systems. We can't only treat our bodies. We must consider our whole selves: soul, body, mind. We need to treat our emotions — anger, hurt, resentment, feelings of helplessness and fear. Forgiveness is crucial in the recovery process. Although it is hard work, it is worth it. I chose life so I can teach so many things to my children and, most importantly, see them grow up.

My mind was still processing what the surgeon told me and the myriad tests to complete after our return to Europe, when we walked by a lingerie store.

> "Why don't you go in and buy some nice, sexy
> lingerie for yourself?" Paul said.

I could not believe it. *Who is this person?* I just had surgery and was diagnosed with a chronic disease. More tests and surgery awaited, and all he could think of was sex? *God, something is very wrong here.* I thought. I had to get as far away as possible from this person I hardly recognized anymore. On the other hand, I needed to get physically and emotionally stronger before I could divorce him. I had to be patient.

We flew back to Europe where my blood tests and CT scans were completed. They were all good and my çolonoscopy test was also negative — they did not find anything abnormal. Even though everything seemed OK, the oncologist still recommended the surgery, which I did not completely understand. However, two doctors in two different countries with excellent medical systems made the same recommendations. They must be right, and I have to do it, I thought. I knew little about the surgery and the possible consequences and complications. Although they explained everything to me, I did not think that any of it could happen to me, so I paid little attention to it.

My right hemicolectomy surgery was scheduled for August 28th, 2015. I wasn't nervous about it, and according to the surgeon everything went well. However, the first night after my surgery something was off. The next morning when they did blood tests, they discovered something was very wrong. The surgeon said my blood test result "didn't make sense." He ordered a CT scan, which showed that my intestines were bleeding. The surgeon said another surgery was necessary to stop it. I immediately felt I was being pulled down by something so strong and powerful that I could hardly resist. It was like a vortex. I fought so hard to stay on top of it and not be sucked into this deep, dark hole. I didn't know what it was, but it took tremendous effort to fight it off. I knew I was fighting for my life. My body started to shake very heavily. It was shutting down and giving up. My body had suffered too much and lost a significant amount of blood.

My last thought was *I'm not going to make it*. I was terrified beyond words. My fear was overwhelming. I was rushed into the operating room in August 29th, 2015 where I spent about four hours in surgery and received a blood transfusion. I don't remember anything about the surgery. I had no special encounter of white light, Angels or a tunnel as others describe about near-death experiences. I had accepted the fact that this was the end. Except it wasn't.

My time had not come yet.

The doctors and my surgeon said I was very "lucky." I like to think that it was more than luck. I have received tremendous help from Higher Realms to stay alive and complete my mission on this planet.

When I got out of the operating room, Paul said I looked like I had aged twenty years. I was hooked up to various machines when I woke up from the anesthesia in the Intensive Care Unit. I had tubes entering and leaving my body in several ways. One was running through my nose and connected to my colon in my lower abdomen to clear out blood from my intestines. I spent three days and nights in ICU.

After I was cleared to leave ICU, I was transferred to the hospital for three weeks. I had a private room with a big television and a private washroom. Lunches were like healthy, delicious multi-course meals from a five-star restaurant. Initially, I could not eat much so my children ate most of my lunches when they came to visit me. It was a modern, well-equipped clinic with a holistic approach. While lying in the clinic, many health care professionals visited me: a dietician, a physiotherapist, my surgeon, my oncologist, a massage therapist, the hospital's doctors and nurses, even a priest. I also had a few meetings with the clinical psychologist. I told her about my frustration with the surgeon and how I was looking for answers as to how I almost died.

I picked up an infection, so I received intravenous antibiotics three times a day in my arms. The spot where the IV entered was swollen and covered with green and blue bruises. Toward the end of the treatment, the IV was removed because my arm looked terrible. I received morphine for the intense physical pain. I had night sweats and often had to change my soaking wet pajamas in the middle of the night.

I was puzzled and angry with the doctors and the surgeon. *How could this happen?* I almost died from a surgery I wasn't even sure was necessary. I had so many blaming thoughts racing in my mind while I was lying in the hospital. I accept now that the surgery was necessary in medical terms to see whether the cancer had metastasized in my lymphatic system, but it was tough to accept at the time. After my surgery, they checked over thirty lymph nodes under a microscope and only found one with cancerous cells, which was great news. Today I'm grateful for the team of excellent doctors, nurses, surgeons and health care professionals who took care of me in the hospital and helped me recover physically. I realized that all these painful, "negative" experiences were the beginning of something greater and better, but it was an intensely difficult time.

After facing death, my fear of dying slowly dissolved then disappeared. I no longer fear it like I once did. I even had a conversation with my children about death and the afterlife. This experience made it clear that I had to change my life drastically. I was not prepared to die that day in the hospital.

I was hoping that after this distressing experience Paul would change and be kind with me. This was not the case. He was unable to show emotional support. We had an argument a few days after I got home from the hospital. I was still very weak, but he was strong enough to defend his point of view. Like when I broke my elbow, he did not help much with the kids or around the house. Once again, my mom looked after the kids for weeks until I recovered.

These were strong messages from the Universe, God/Goddess and Angels to change my life. It was *time* to wake up from my nightmare. Up to that point I had lived my life unconsciously. Others made decisions for me and controlled my life.

So, I woke up.

I gradually turned my life around. I began the process of ending my miserable relationship, recovered from my surgeries and disease, changed my lifestyle and rebuilt my life with my two children. I regained my freedom, independence and power by making conscious choices. Finally, I got rid of fear, anger and resentment. I have achieved peace, love and happiness in my heart.

Are you ready to wake up and take back control over your life? Or would you prefer living unconsciously and unaware? You decide!

Chapter Eight

My Spiritual Awakening and Journey: My Lifestyle Changes

Something started the day I was diagnosed with my disease or the day when I faced death. These two wake-up calls changed my life forever. My life will never be the same, and I can't go back — not like I wanted to go back. I was waking up and it felt great.

In *The Tibetan Book of Living and Dying* (2002), Sogyal Rinpoche says the Earth is full of suffering and pain, and that this is a catalyst for spiritual change. The reason for all adversities such as loss, grief and disappointment in people's lives is "to wake us up" and help us break free from endless misery and "release our imprisoned splendor" (p.118).

I felt so blessed to get another chance. I was sincerely grateful to continue my life consciously toward my spiritual transformation. Slowly, I started to change my life by making my own decisions and following through with actions. Louise Hay's books[4] helped me immensely. Through her recommendations, I created my first list of positive affirmation statements in 2016. I used statements such as, "I live a joyous, happy, fulfilling, healthy, loving life with many kind people around me," "I'm guided by my higher self and by Angels," "I love myself and I'm loved," "I deserve the best," "I'm in perfect health and abundant energy flows freely in my body".

While I was doing my "research" at home, I had regular blood work and CT scans at the hospital. I stayed home for about a year after my surgeries. Then I returned to work and continued my part-time job while recovering and living with a terrible pain. For a few years after my surgeries I had severe discomfort on and off in my bladder. Sometimes it lasted for hours, sometimes for days. Often, I could not sleep as I had to wake up ten times a night to use the washroom. I thought it was somehow connected to my surgeries, so I saw a few medical specialists. They conducted tests but found nothing abnormal. After a few months I just accepted it and learned to live with the pain. I believe my body was trying to send me messages (i.e., take back control over my life and end my marriage) through this discomforting bladder pain. Today I no longer have bladder pain like I used to have and I can sleep through the night (although occasionally I still experience slight discomfort when I'm stressed). I don't know for sure, but I believe

---

[4]   Louise Hay: *Meditations to Heal Your Life*, Hay House, 1994
    Louise Hay: *You Can Heal Your Life*, Hay House, 1984

the lifestyle changes I made over the years positively influenced my bladder condition. I am so relieved to be free from that torment.

One step at a time, I told myself.

First, I focused on my nutrition and slowly transitioned to a mainly plant-based diet. I prepared a list with special vegetables, fruits and spices and another list with all the food I should be avoiding, and I placed it on my fridge. It was a good reminder every day what I should be and should not be eating. Try it — it helped me a lot. I have been vegetarian since January 2017. Although I'm not 100% vegan, I'm doing my best to eliminate most dairy products from my diet. I also eliminated most processed food and decreased my sugar consumption. Being too strict and setting high expectations did not work — I tried it and failed. Vegetarian and vegan diets are not for everyone. I used to eat everything — all kinds of meat, milk, yoghurt, cheese, bread, dessert, pastries, cakes, ice cream, etc. — so I needed to take it slowly.

The key is to make gradual changes and find the right balance until you reach an optimal diet you are comfortable with and that best supports your body. When I have cravings (especially for sugar) I eat an ice cream or homemade dessert without feeling guilty about it. As part of my diet change, I bought a juicer to make my own carrot, apple, orange and green juices. At first, it was tiring and time consuming but now it is part of my routine. My children also benefit from my dietary changes (I have introduced lots of new, healthy foods and desserts in their diet and they drink freshly squeezed juice regularly) and I have noticed they get sick less often in the last few years.

Rethinking how I eat has been an overwhelming and long process. It is not easy. There is no right or wrong way because it is different for everyone. This process took about five years for me, and it is not yet done. I continually try new recipes, attend cooking courses, adjust my diet and read new books on nutrition. There are plenty of wonderful books and free recipes on the internet if you are interested in changing your diet. I'm not a nutritionist or dietary expert so I won't advise you to follow any specific diet, but generally it is a good idea to cut down on sugar and processed food and increase your daily vegetable and fruit consumption. It is also a good idea to consult with health care professionals and a nutritionist. You must figure out what works for you and fits into your schedule.

In addition to my diet changes, I added daily walks to get fresh air and regular exercise into my weekly schedule. I bought a treadmill and started yoga classes. Since 2016 I have been doing a great variety of activities such as running, biking, swimming, skiing, skating, a group weight-training class, yoga, walking and dancing. It never gets boring.

Later I bought books on mindfulness and how to reduce stress. I have focused my mind on releasing resentment and anger I have carried for years. Furthermore, I regularly repeat positive statements and express gratitude for all I have. I have discovered that when I'm sad, dancing and listening to music always cheers me up. Singing also helps me release stress and overcome a difficult day. Finally, any kind of sport, meditation and nature walks are excellent at reducing tension and raising my spirit.

Lately, my attention shifted to spirituality. I attended a big spiritual festival and a spiritual retreat. I have been watching lots of spiritual movies and documentaries, as well as reading books. I practice meditation and yoga frequently.

My "transformation" started after my surgeries in 2015. It is an ongoing process and requires discipline and relentless practice. As a result of my shift, everything and everyone around me started to change as well.

Changes have been incremental but significant between 2015 and 2020:

- My face and skin are more vibrant and radiant.
- My hair has returned to its natural beauty after I stopped colouring it.
- I shop less.
- I complain, gossip and argue less.
- I stopped watching the news.
- I have more energy.
- I live in the present. My mind is no longer preoccupied with the past or the future.
- I spread kindness everywhere I go and often smile at people.
- I exercise regularly.
- People open up to me and tell me about their problems, which I appreciate.
- I help everywhere I can.
- Meditation and yoga are part of my life.
- I'm no longer afraid of death and dying.
- I'm more balanced and grounded.
- My self-love and self-acceptance have increased significantly.
- I feel people's energy. I sense things. My intuitive ability has been heightened.
- I attracted new like-minded friends while my old friends disappeared from my life.
- I learned to say "No." I grew up and was socialized into a family and society where women don't often say no. I had to learn how to say no to Paul, my children, my mom or my manager without feeling guilty about it.

At first all these changes will be extremely hard and occasionally frustrating. It is challenging to break old patterns and habits, but anything is possible with *persistence, repetition and determination.* As the saying goes, persistence pays off. Once it becomes part of your routine, you will love it and you won't go back to your previous lifestyle.

If you are planning to make *conscious choices* about your life, you need to rewire old patterns in your brain and establish new, helpful and positive patterns which ultimately lead to more aware choices about your relationships, your diet, your job and your goals. In practice this could mean repeating empowering affirmations, accessing universal consciousness (and your higher self) through meditation, changing your subconscious belief system or listening to your intuition and feelings instead of following your mind.

Look at your diet, lifestyle, physical activities, relationships, job, marriage, business, emotional health, hobbies and how you spend your free time. Make a list of what you want to change and then take actions. It is up to you. Maybe you are already eating healthy and exercise regularly, but you have a stressful job. Consider working on stress relief or finding another job. Maybe you have a job you love but you eat unhealthily and don't exercise. Or maybe you are in an unhappy relationship and don't do much for your emotional and mental health. Figure out what is holding you back and decide to make changes.

If you really want to change you will find the time, the money, and the solution. Even if you are super busy you can always find ten minutes for a walk in the fresh air, five minutes for meditation and five minutes to prepare a quick, healthy salad. Instead of watching TV or using computer, take half an hour every day to do something for your health. On the weekend you can do significantly more. You can go biking, swimming, running, or dancing with friends. Do something that makes you feel good and is healthy. It is no more complicated or time-consuming to prepare a healthy than an unhealthy meal. Find a few good recipes — there are hundreds on the internet — and try them. *Practice* is an important word: the changes don't just happen. We have to practice and repeat these new, healthy choices until they become part of our routine. We must be committed and disciplined.

Everybody's life circumstances are different, and you are the only one who knows what you need to have a happy, healthy and balanced life. Don't let anybody criticize your new lifestyle. Don't let others mitigate *your efforts for change.*

It is your life, your decisions, your lessons, your journey!

Chapter Nine

Separation and Divorce

*"I think the first step is to understand that
forgiveness does not exonerate the perpetrator.
Forgiveness liberates the victim.
It's a gift you give yourself."*
T.D. Jakes

In the summer of 2017, we moved once again due to Paul's job. We were back in my home country where everything started and would end between us. The Universe has a fascinating way of arranging things. It is like a cycle with repetitive patterns. As strange as it sounds, it feels like I repeated and reproduced the same living conditions over and over in these countries until I broke the pattern. There were many similarities in the way we lived in these countries and also how I felt. I created the same reality and the same problems with small variations in different places. I thought that moving to a new country and having another job would change everything. It didn't. It is like a default mode: I attracted the same boring job, experienced the same problems in my relationship no matter what I did. I had the same responsibilities regarding taking care of my children and the household chores. It was time to create *a new reality for myself.*

We practically lived two separate lives in one house. Paul worked late and was always busy. He went to the gym and work-related receptions in the evenings. He started to eat alone in a café three or four times a week in the mornings. A few months later he began eating his breakfast in the same coffee shop every morning. When I mentioned that we should be eating together as a family once a week, he said no. So, I took the kids to the playground most Sunday mornings while he had his breakfast. Sometimes the kids saw him sitting in the café and waved at him when we walked to the playground.

I created an "independent" life I enjoyed by leaving Paul out as much as I could. In my free time I regularly went to the theatre and watched comedy, drama, opera and musicals. Sometimes I went out to dance or have dinner with my friends. I organized my children's activities, drove them to swimming lessons after school, and took my daughter to ballet on Saturday mornings. A few months after our arrival I accepted a three-month full-time job in an office. Once again, I had no time for myself and for all the things I had been diligently and persistently doing for my health. Often the fridge was empty when I got home from work and the kids got home from school. My job was stressful and demanding, so I decided to stop compromising my health and well-being for money or a career. I would not go back to the overworked, exhausted, unhappy, emotionally and physically sick life I once led. I knew better. Although I was offered another contract, I did not accept it.

Instead I decided to accomplish some of the soul-supporting activities I had waited for a long time to do. Being kind with other people empowers us and makes us feel wonderful, so I volunteered and did some charity work. I spent time helping the teachers and students in my kids' classrooms. I organized events and games for the kids at Halloween and Christmas, which I loved and kept me busy. I collected donations — toys, clothes, food and money — for foster homes and delivered them in person. Every time I visited the foster home and handed over toys to the children it felt great. Finally, I taught English in a high school for unprivileged students in a poor neighbourhood. Although I don't have a teacher's degree, I'm passionate about teaching. These seventeen- to eighteen-year-old kids were very eager to learn English, so I encouraged them to talk and gave them lots of positive feedback, which they appreciated.

Even though I was not paid, I did something I loved while helping other human beings. These were the most rewarding jobs of my life. It is important to note that *giving and receiving* is part of the same cycle: you can't always receive without giving and you can't only give without receiving. They are both equally important.

In the summer of 2018, I visited a large outdoor spiritual festival attended by hundreds of people. On the first day, I joined a small group of people who listened to a speech about sexuality. I don't remember the details of the presentation, but I identified with everything the speaker said. At the end of the speech she asked every one of us to hug five people. Those hugs were incredibly powerful and filled me with lots of positive energy. That is how my day started at the festival.

I stayed for two days and felt like a curious child: I was interested in everything, I was inquisitive, I was smiling at everyone and talking to many people. I believe my inner child felt happy for the first time in a long time. I listened to many fascinating lectures: one was held by a shaman; another one was about tantra. I did group meditation, yoga and free dance. The next day I woke up early, so I was at the festival location by 6:00 a.m. I met a man on my way, and we walked together to an early meditation. While walking, we laughed non-stop: it was like something was in the air; we could not stop smiling and giggling like two children. We did two hours of mantra meditation together then said goodbye. I ate delicious vegan meals and I bought my first healing crystal bracelets with lapis lazuli, amethyst, citrine, hematite, rose quartz, tiger eye and clear quartz. Later, I went to a concert where six people played different instruments magnificently. I was captivated. While listening to the beautiful voice of the female lead singer I looked around and saw a utopian world in the warm, sunny day. Peaceful and smiling people walking by, children playing on the swings, dogs running around off leash. There was a lake in the background and lots of trees around us. Overflowing positive energy and a high vibration filled the air and the space. After these two days it was difficult to return to my reality and my everyday life. I was highly energized and enthusiastic when I got home. Paul was watching a soccer game and he hardly looked up when I entered the room. I remember I wanted to share my amazing experience with somebody so much, but I couldn't. Paul was not interested at all.

Once I started my spiritual journey and meditated more, the gap between Paul's energy and mine became wider. I was often at a high frequency level while Paul stayed at his low, often depleted energy level. It was so obvious that we were miles apart and that one day this marriage would end.

That day came.

I'm proud and feel empowered that I broke out of my marriage and recreated my reality. I also broke my parents' pattern and chose another path. Many people unconsciously follow their parents' pattern and even repeat some of their mistakes because it is all they know. By default, I attracted a husband who had many similarities with my father. In my childhood, my brain was conditioned in a way (i.e., I'm not worthy, I'm not loved and I'm not good enough) because my father never showed me any love or affection. Therefore, this was so familiar that later, as an adult, it was normal for me to stay in the same unloving situation for years. Only when I became conscious enough and was able to rewire old patterns of my brain and replace them with new ones (i.e., I am worthy, I am loved, and I am good enough) could I make a different choice and move away from the emotionally abusive environment.

I no longer believed in the institution of marriage, and I did not want to meet anyone's expectations anymore. I certainly did not want to feel obliged *to do or not do something because of my marriage.* You see? I chose freedom, joy and happiness without restrictions, obligations or expectations.

People exchange vows and promise to be faithful, support each other in sickness and in health and to, essentially, be on each other's side. What happens to those promises? Most of them — if not all — are broken over the years. As I wrote earlier, a marriage can restrict a person in many ways. People often supress their desires, which ultimately makes them suffer. On the other hand, if they satisfy their desires, they suffer in lies and guilt or they end up in a bitter divorce.

People are often under pressure from family, friends, society and the church. Single women in their 30s (or in their 20s in some societies) are expected to get married, have children and raise them within marriage even if this marriage is broken beyond repair like mine. Why so much pressure and so many expectations? This is the twenty-first century.

Everybody has a choice. It is OK to have children or not. It is OK to get married or stay single. It is OK to divorce or stay married for many years. It is OK to raise your children as a single parent or in a relationship.

No expectations! No judgment! No obligations!

Every one of us has the right to decide how to live our lives. Every one of us creates experiences we want in our lives. Free choices. Free will. That is all we have, and it was given to us.

I chose to get married and have children because I wanted to. In the same respect, I chose to divorce and raise my children as a single mom when I realized my marriage was slowly "destroying" my soul and everything inside me. I do not regret marrying Paul or divorcing him. Both were my choices.

In September 2018 I told Paul I wanted a divorce. This decision was the result of many years of thinking, analyzing options and intense emotional struggle. As a woman and mother, it was not easy to walk away from a marriage with two children. I invested an extraordinary amount of energy and time to create a safe, comfortable home for my family. The children had just started school, so we decided to wait until the end of the school year before moving back to Canada in the summer. The next few months were tough. I told Paul there would be no sex anymore, and that I wouldn't go on a planned ski vacation with him either. That angered him very much, but I had to be resilient and strong.

Paul reached his breaking point on Christmas morning. He said he would end his contract, and we would not wait until summer but move back to Canada in the winter. I agreed. This relationship had been in distress for both of us for a long time. I told the kids everything. I could not lie to them and keep it secret. While I was talking to them, Paul was lying in bed looking distressed and deeply troubled. He did not say a word, but he looked extremely disturbed. I explained to the children that we were going to move back to Canada and live separately. They remembered little of Canada as we had lived overseas for five years. I also said we both loved them the same and they would see Daddy regularly while living with me. I remained astonishingly calm while talking to the children. The peace surrounding us was incredible and indescribable. I'm grateful for the support of the Angels and the positive energy coming from Higher Realms that helped us through that intense moment.

Paul was full of hatred — I had never seen him like that before. I could not be around him, so I packed up and took the kids to my parents' house in the countryside on December 25th, 2018. The next day Paul called and asked me to stay until summer as we originally planned. It turned out he did not really want a divorce. He was very angry because I refused to have sex with him and go on the ski vacation.

On December 26th he sent me a long email saying he felt sorry because he failed me as a husband, and he let me and the kids down. He always thought that we had a responsibility to the children to stay together "no matter the cost." He wrote that he was worried about how difficult our lives would be without him after our separation, and that I had to manage all the burden alone while knowing that the kids and I would need his help. He continued saying that he felt terrible when he thought about how much hardship I would face without any support network upon my return to Canada.

I was determined to get rid of my "victim identity" and feeling weak and dependent. In *You Can Heal Yourself* (1984), Louise Hay tells us that the Universe supports us in our feelings of helplessness if we choose those thoughts. She also emphasizes that as long as we feel like a victim and blame others for our problems, we are not in charge of our life because we have given away our power (p.1, 7, 29). I decided to take back my power from Paul and master my life based on my intuition and guided by my spirit.

I had to be strong and get away from him for real and forever. There was *no way back* for me. The "cost" (as he put it) of staying with him for the sake of our children was already too high for me. So, I was resilient. It was the most difficult ten days of my life. He was always a great manipulator. He tried everything to convince me to stay. He was like a rollercoaster. One day he was nice to me, the next he was arrogant and overpowering. He put a lot of pressure on me. It was emotionally exhausting, but I knew no matter what he did or said I wasn't going back to him. I remained firm in my decision. I made it clear I was not going home until he formally informed his manager about our divorce and our intention to return to Canada. I waited for ten days before he finally sent the email. It was a huge relief.

I returned home with the kids and started to organize everything before our big move. It took me about eight weeks before everything was sorted out and packed so we could fly back to Canada. During this time, we had to negotiate our separation agreement. Paul was being unreasonable, so I decided to hire lawyers in Canada to protect my interests and draft the agreement. Paul tried to convince me that I didn't need a lawyer because it was a waste of money (as he said) and that he could write the separation agreement. For a day or two I even believed him. After a few days I realized that no matter the costs for a lawyer, it was an absolute must. Of course, money was not the real reason why he did not want me to have a lawyer. He did not want anybody to represent me so he could retain control over me and the divorce process to serve his interests. Paul and his controlling personality made everything difficult for me. When things did not go his way, like when I hired my lawyers, he felt threatened and became very hostile. I was the target of all his rage, hurt and pain. Although I was still a bit vulnerable, I no longer felt like a victim thanks to my two female lawyers' support.

No divorce is easy, but ours went beyond my imagination. If you decide to end your marriage, you may be in for a tough and messy fight. A divorce can bring out the worst in people, especially if — like Paul — they do not want it. He created lots of fear inside me about my future. *He wanted me to believe that I couldn't manage my life without him.* This is not to scare you but to prepare you. You need to stay strong and confident. Most importantly, don't let your spouse scare you. You also need good lawyers to navigate the divorce process.

My priority was to sign the agreement as fast as possible, keep the lawyers' costs to a minimum and not prolong the process. Negotiating the agreement with Paul was extremely challenging. My instincts told me I couldn't return to Canada without a signed separation agreement, so my lawyers prepared it. His arrogance shone through when he told me that since he didn't need a lawyer, I should pay for everything. He wouldn't contribute to the costs of drafting the agreement, so I paid for everything. It was expensive, but I don't regret it. The agreement included the custody arrangement of our children, the financial settlement and the monthly support payments, so it was an important legal document. I no longer wanted to be dependent on him after returning to Canada because I knew I would be on my own to look after our two children and he would be busy with his own issues. I wanted to make sure that the agreement settled everything so I could focus solely on the kids' well-being and make sure they were comfortable and integrating well into the new school and country.

It was a tough negotiation and a stressful process, but it had to be done. I'm grateful for my two wonderful lawyers' assistance in this process. I prayed every day and asked for the Angels' help to settle it quickly. A few weeks before our flight to Canada, Paul signed the agreement. I was FREE.

Chapter Ten

A New Beginning: Free, Independent, Strong Me

"To forgive is to set a prisoner free and
discover that the prisoner was you."
Lewis B. Smedes

It was an ecstatic and blissful feeling to be free, independent and in control of my life again. Divorcing Paul was the most significant, influential and best decision I have ever made. I had hit *rock bottom* so hard that it felt like it did not matter what happened to me, that things couldn't get worse and that my life could only get better. I reached a point where *I no longer feared uncertainty and the unknown.* I was willing to leave my comfortable life and financial security behind because my well-being and that of my children were vastly more important. My spiritual development, following my heart and strengthening my soul took precedence over material comforts.

There were many uncertainties and unknowns, but I knew everything would be all right. It felt wonderful knowing that I no longer had to move around due to Paul's job, and I could finally settle down. There were some risks; for example, whether I would be able to find and buy a home because there are so few properties on the market in the winter in Canada and I had limited financial resources. I did not have a job or a car. I did not have much family (other than my cousin) or friends for support and I did not know much about the schools.

I had to build everything from zero. Although I had done it many times as we moved around, I had never done it alone with two kids. On one hand, I was dependent on Paul. On the other hand, I always quickly explored everything in the new country. I'm extremely adaptable and resilient. We received lots of support from Paul's employer in the past moves, but this time I was on my own and I was OK with it.

I was ready to leave my comfort zone behind and leap into the unknown. I also learned that this was the only way for my soul to evolve. Moving back to Canada alone with two young children was a huge decision, but it was the right one. This move showed me that anything is possible no matter how hard it seems. It increased my personal power and built my confidence. Canada feels more like home to me than the country I was born in or anywhere else we lived over the years.

Our lives could truly begin again. The Universe supported me, and I was no longer afraid. Learning to live without fear is one of the keys that changed my life, but belief was just as important. I trusted the Universe, Angels and God/Goddess to help me and give me everything we needed. I discovered that when I *replace my fear with trust*, I can do anything. This was when I started to live.

After five years in Europe, we returned to Canada on February 19th, 2019. It was a typical chilly, windy day. My mom flew with me and supported me as always. She was to stay with us in Canada for a few weeks while I got organized. Paul took a taxi from the airport to his downtown hotel leaving me and my mother with two exhausted, hungry kids and ten big suitcases at the airport. That was *harsh.*

Ellie — my cousin who had been living in Canada for a long time — was waiting at the airport to pick us up. We had so much luggage that we could not fit into one car, so I took a taxi with my kids. Our temporary accommodation was not ideal, but it worked until I bought my own place. We did not have warm blankets, so Ellie brought us some. She cooked us food and made us feel welcome. The next day she drove us to a grocery store. Since our shipment of furniture and clothing would not arrive for two months, she took us to places to buy everything we needed. In the first few weeks my mom and Ellie helped me so much.

Before moving to Canada, I wrote a list with many positive affirmations. Try it — it worked for me. One of them was: "I buy a beautiful, spacious condo in Canada close to the school. It has big windows, a balcony, a fitness room and kind neighbours." Within a few weeks I found the perfect one. It had been on the market for a while and even the agent said she didn't understand why it hadn't sold. I knew why: it was "reserved" for me. The price was perfect. It was exactly how much money I received in our financial arrangement. I did not negotiate; I accepted the price and bought the condo. The location is perfect. It is walking distance to the school, which turned out to be one of the best ranked in the city. It is walking distance to playgrounds, bike paths, parks, the library, grocery stores and the river. The two-bedroom layout is perfect; one of the bedrooms is very spacious so the kids can share it. Our living room is full of natural light, as I imagined, and the building has a swimming pool and a treadmill. *Perfect*, I thought.

The Universe took care of everything we needed. It is like everything was organized and arranged in the perfect order. Paul and I registered the kids at the school and got their health cards done in the first week. On their first day of school there was a big snowstorm, so we waited for forty minutes for the taxi, which made them late. After that, I quickly bought a small used car and a cell phone. Within two months I had a condo, a car and the kids settled into school. I had everything I imagined and wrote down on my list before arriving in Canada.

The kids and I gradually settled into our new home and life. We moved into our new apartment in the spring. Paul painted the kids' room and put the furniture together. I decorated the rooms, and a Feng Shui expert helped me create a simple, harmonious, calm place filled with positive energy. I keep my apartment clutter-free and clean. Before moving in I sold and donated lots of clothes, furniture, toys and jewelry. I got rid of lots of useless stuff, and I feel so much better. One of the only issues is that the building is located on a busy and noisy street. Pollution, noise and dust in our apartment is problematic at times. The kids also needed time to get used to a shared room. Now they love it. Mia said the new apartment feels more like home than any of our previous huge houses.

The kids like the new school and their teachers. One of the best things is that we can walk to school, unlike before when the kids had to spend an hour on the school bus every day. Mia said to me one day, "Mommy, I'm looking forward to going to school." She had never said that before. Mia's health class had a "twenty-one-day mindfulness challenge" where they were taught how to use mindfulness and positive affirmations. They also learned about forgiveness, practical strategies to calm themselves and how to control anxiety. She loved this class. She has a solid foundation because I have been teaching her about spirituality and affirmations for the last five years. Isn't this wonderful? I wish every school had similar classes so a new generation of children would grow up as self-loving, confident, aware, independent, happy adults with less fear, anxiety and worry. I smile when I think that the Universe chose the perfect school for my children.

Being single and independent comes with more responsibilities. It also means doing things I haven't done before. I negotiated with the real estate agent, insurance broker, car dealer, internet providers, lawyers and banks. I need to take my car for gas, servicing and tire changes. I need to pay my bills and manage my finances. Often, I need to call a tradesperson to fix something in my condo. It has all been part of my learning process toward full independence.

I noticed that my thinking patterns have changed too. When we first lived in Canada for seven years, I complained a lot about the long, harsh, snowy, frigid winter. The winter is still the same — sometimes the temperature drops to -30°C with strong wind gusts. There are big snowstorms and winter lasts from October to the end of March. But my reaction has changed. Instead of complaining I organize outdoor activities like skating and skiing. The kids love walking to school in the snow and playing and sledding down huge "snow mountains." It's a matter of perspective: we can choose to complain about the snow, cold and difficult driving conditions and isolate ourselves in our homes for four or five months, or we can take advantage of the snow by exploring new and fun adventures. This is true for everything. We have the power to decide how to react to an issue. We can create a pleasant experience instead of suffering and complaining. All it takes is to change our approach and the way we think about it. Try it. Think of something you don't like and shift your approach about it.

According to our separation agreement I'm the primary caregiver for our children. It means the kids are always with me except Sundays between 10:00 a.m. and 5:00 p.m., and Wednesday evening for two hours. When we signed the agreement, we did not even consider a 50-50 co-parenting arrangement, which is the norm in Canada. After two months, I wanted a weekend off and a night alone, so I asked Paul to take the kids so I could go out to dance and have a "child free" weekend. He refused. He wanted me to get a job and renegotiate the financial arrangement. I explained that having a job had nothing to do with my free weekend, and that finding a suitable job takes time. I made it clear that I would no longer work in an environment I wasn't happy in, and I would no longer do a job I didn't like. He didn't care much about what I did or whether I liked it; he just wanted me to work so he could pay me less support.

No more compromise for me. We had just arrived, and I wanted to make sure the children were comfortable and settled before I started my job search. I reminded him that I supported his career for over a decade and moved around the world many times with him. I reminded him I was raising the children, had worked part-time and did domestic work while he built his career and got promoted. Now it was his turn to support me until I found an appropriate job. I tried to reason with him and asked him to accommodate the children for one night a month, but it was hopeless. One of his e-mails (sent on May 5th, 2019) essentially said, I'm not responsible for your fun.

Slowly I accepted it and I surrendered. I practised nonresistance which meant I would not argue with him anymore, so I did not have a free evening or weekend for three months. Because of my lawyers' foresight, the agreement equally distributed holidays and long weekends between Paul and I, so as per the agreement he had to take the kids for the first long weekend. Finally, after three months I had my first free weekend: for the first time in a long time I went out to a club alone. I was overjoyed and excited; I could do whatever I wanted freely. I danced all night and met some kind people. The bliss of being free (after seventeen years) can not be compared to anything I had felt for a long time. It was a truly ecstatic feeling and I had so much fun.

Although I had very few free evenings, it seemed that *the whole Universe conspired to help me go out and have fun*. I had another free night the next month and so on. Paul's efforts to prevent me from going out and meeting new people failed.

I discovered I am no longer "searching." I no longer live in the past or the future. I stopped "wanting and needing more," which was a turning point in my life. We live in a wonderful, safe country with kind people around us. We have a comfortable apartment and a car. We have food and clothes. My children go to a great school and do sport and fun activities. I can pay the bills. I live a fit lifestyle with regular exercise and a healthy diet. I realized I have everything I need and want.

Around October 2019, Paul agreed to look after the children two nights a month, so I started to go out to regular clubs, which was a different world after visiting adult clubs for years. I have discovered a night club with amazing live music. At first it was strange to go out alone as a single woman. Now I love it. Sometimes I dance alone, which I enjoy as much as dancing with others. People are often drawn to me. Dancing and music energize and transform me. It is a transcendent experience that I adore.

Dating as a single mom is different from when I last dated almost twenty years ago. I know what I want, which makes it so much easier. Luckily, my looks haven't changed a lot (except for few wrinkles and few grey hairs). I'm in better shape now than twenty years ago as a result of my healthy lifestyle. I'm very fit and I have natural, long brown hair. When I met my husband, my number one priority was to have children. This time I just want to have fun. Becoming a single parent and divorcing Paul changed everything. I no longer spend my time with someone I'm not attracted to or I'm not comfortable with. When meeting somebody, I enjoy each moment. Every compliment feels wonderful. Touching, kissing and having an intimate relationship feels more pleasurable.

I signed up for online dating sites and started to meet men for coffee on Sundays, my free day. Online dating is a whole new world to me as well. Initially, I was excited about every meeting and interested in every person's life story and their ongoing search for love. A year later, I rarely use these sites anymore. Honestly, I prefer traditional face-to-face meetings and real-life experiences over online.

On New Year's Eve of 2019 I went out with Ellie and her husband. There were hundreds of people at the night club: women dressed up in shiny, glittery dresses, some wearing shimmering multicoloured hats. There were long line-ups at the bars to order a drink, but in the big crowd I noticed someone. He noticed me too. He approached me and we started to talk. We danced then kissed at midnight. When we kissed on the dance floor, I felt a shift of energy, something strong and massive. When I told him this, he said, "I think everybody around us felt it." It was like a romantic movie, except for the happy ending. A few days later we met for a coffee and decided to spend the day together because we enjoyed each other's company so much. We exchanged lots of text messages every day, and it turned out we had a lot in common: we had both travelled a lot around the world and lived in different cities. We liked the same music and similar food.

A few weeks later he invited me to dinner at his place. I was excited and took a lot of time to prepare for my date. I had professional makeup done and bought a bottle of quality red wine for him. There was a big snowstorm in the evening, so I decided to call a taxi. He made dinner and a delicious cocktail for me. I could not remember the last time a man prepared a meal for me. After dinner, we went out to dance. I felt great with him: always smiling, joyous and energized. It was a perfect evening. At the end of the night he dropped me off in front of my building at 2:00 a.m. and quickly drove away, which I thought was very odd. I desperately searched for my key to get into the warm building. It was extremely windy and cold — about -20°C — and I was wearing a dress with tights. When I got up to my apartment and sat down, I could not move for about twenty minutes. Thoughts were racing in my mind. What did I do? What did I say? I felt and knew I wouldn't see him ever again. For weeks I tried to understand what happened and why he walked away. I was frustrated with the Universe and the Angels and kept asking questions like, "Why did he show up in my life?" and "Why did you take him away from me so quickly?" *It is not fair*, I thought. I had such a good time with him.

Eventually I realized I don't have to understand the "why." I just have to accept that either he was not the right person, or the timing wasn't right yet. Later, I sent him a text message wishing him good luck with finding the partner he is looking for and to be happy with. I'm confident that one day I will find my soulmate whom I can laugh with and share my love with.

Chapter Eleven

My Family: My Parents and My Children

My father was taken to the hospital while I was writing my book. His mental and physical health has been deteriorating for years, he can't move much and can't remember things. He falls asleep every twenty minutes while sitting at the table. It feels like only his body is here. He mistreated himself by consuming huge amounts of alcohol and eating unhealthy food all his life. He is overweight and doesn't do any exercise. He has high blood pressure and high blood sugar. He is on many different medications. He lived his whole life filled with fury, anger, rage and fear. Even though he looked strong and confident outside, he was scared and insecure inside.

Unfortunately, I could not visit him in the hospital because I'm far away. I prayed and sent him love and energy. I also asked the Angels to help him remain calm and release his fear and anxiety. He was released from the hospital after a week. I'm not sure how much time is left for him in this world, as I believe his organs are struggling to keep his body alive. I called him one day and thanked him for all he had done for me over the years even though I know he was not the perfect father. I said, "I know you did the best you could with the knowledge you had in that time, and for that I'm very grateful." I also told him that I feel fantastic after my separation, and he does not have to worry about me anymore. I think he felt relief after our conversation.

My mother feels like a friend I can turn to any time. Over the years I shared a lot with her about my difficulties with Paul. She was always there for me and constantly supported me. However, we had many conflicts about her manipulations (which she does not even notice) and about my children for many years. I was often angry with her when she tried to prove to me and my children how "perfect" she is while telling me what I should be doing differently. Sometimes she made me feel like I'm "not good enough." Although I'm grateful for her help, she needed to accept that I raise my children the way I think is best, and I'm doing the best I can. She spoils them of course: she buys them everything, she can't say no to them and serves them excessively as she did with us. I have accepted that is the way she is, which is OK.

At times I have been harsh, impatient and frustrated with her. I apologized to her for that. Although she is prone to judge people and complain a lot, I'm no longer open to listening to her judgemental tone. I don't blame my mom. She was not very conscious about her choices either. I realized how unhappy and hard her life has been with my father. Lately I try to help her transform the way she talks and thinks, and she is changing. I want her to enjoy life and appreciate all she has. Our relationship has significantly improved in the last few years.

As I read in Louise Hay's book, we choose our parents for a reason. She points out that there is no point or need to blame our parents.

Our parents have used their knowledge and their own experiences to raise us in the best possible way, so it is important for us to accept that they did the best they possibly could (*You Can Heal Your Life*, 1984 p.4, 29).

I know I have chosen my parents in order to learn some important lessons on Earth. Both of them had extremely difficult childhoods with little or no love and lots of fear and insecurity. I have accepted that they did their best and there was nothing more they could have done for me. I no longer hold onto past hurts and wounds. I have forgiven them.

My parents

Many parents believe if they stay together in a damaged relationship it is better for the children than divorce. I thought the same. Now I have a different opinion. *Children see and feel everything.* More than we imagine. They know when a mother or father is unhappy. They learn by example and copy what they see around them. Children feel our emotions and our ups-and-downs. I'm amazed how my daughter imitates my mood. When I feel tired and down, she feels the same. When I'm angry, she is angry. When I laugh, dance and sing, she does the same. My son says it is like we are twins. I can't hide anything from her: she senses and detects my feelings with amazing accuracy and reproduces them.

Mia was very angry when I told her and Lyon that I wanted to live separately from their dad. She screamed at me saying, "You ruined my life! You ruined my life!" Now she understands everything. She knows how unhappy I was with her dad, so I had to end the marriage. Lyon was not upset at all. He is a very mature soul. He said, "It's OK, we will see Daddy every week." Mia now accepts that I'm open to a new relationship with a kind, loving, caring person. She even wrote a Soulmate Poem for my birthday:

> "A star that I can see glinting in the sky,
> On a beautiful summer night,
> We finally found each other
> I know it feels right
> We laugh and talk,
> We have our differences,
> Though never drift apart,
> Whatever happens,
> It's true love from the heart."
>
> by Mia

One day I sighed and asked, "When will he show up and when will I meet him?" Lyon overheard it and said, "You have us!" He is right. My children are my biggest treasures. Lyon makes me and Mia laugh all the time. When we talked about marriage and children, he said: "I would like to have sisters and brothers, but I do not want to babysit."

As adults, children follow their parents' patterns unconsciously. Hence a positive role model is crucial in their life. I wanted to show my children that if they feel unhappy in a relationship, they have a choice. They always have a choice. They must accept and learn that nothing in this world is permanent.

Change can bring so many wonderful experiences and new opportunities. Although the first few months were challenging (especially for Mia), my children adjusted so amazingly to a new country, school, apartment and teachers, as well as living separately from their dad. Some parents think their children can't cope with new circumstances. That is not true in my experience. Most children would. Right now, Mia and Lyon have a happy, strong and confident mother, which is the exact opposite of how I was in my marriage. As strange as it sounds, they spend more quality time with their father since we separated than when we lived together. In the winter Paul took the kids to different museums and indoor playhouses. He organizes more outdoor activities with them than ever before: he took the kids biking, skating, skiing and hiking. He also often plays soccer with Lyon and basketball with Mia.

Lyon is a very smart, responsible, confident and kind child with a positive, helpful attitude and calm personality. As his teacher wrote, "He needs to continue to develop his natural leadership skills." He is very active; he enjoys playing soccer, skating and biking in his free time. He has many friends in class. He is a balanced, emotionally and mentally strong spirit and mature soul in the body of a seven-year-old.

Mia is kind, polite and respectful. She has an introverted personality. Her teacher calls her a "discreet member of the classroom," — it took even me a while to understand her temperament. She does not seek attention and often gets exhausted after school. She needs time to process her day and likes being alone. She is a great observer. Mia is very talented and creative: she plays piano and flute brilliantly. She also likes singing and dancing. She loves animals, especially horses. She has a vivid inner world: her drawings of unicorns and fairies are beautiful. She is literally reading all the time. For months she borrowed ten books a week from the library and finished them all by the end of the week. At the age of nine she wrote a fascinating ten-page story.

I'm *blessed* to have them. I'm so proud of them.

Raising children is an exhausting and demanding 24/7 job, therefore it is vital to take a break once in a while. We make "mistakes" and that is OK. We are all learning. Sometimes we push them or ourselves too hard to be the "perfect" parent or the "perfect" child. There is no need to do that. Every child is different and unique. Every child has distinct skills and various interests. Some prefer creative activities over playing sports. Others love sports but are not so keen on reading or math. It is important to allow our children to try different sports, instruments and creative activities so they can decide what to do. Positive reinforcement and praising the children's unique skills can cause miracles and boost their self-confidence. It is also crucial to allow our children to make "mistakes." Finally, children need lots of free time to play and relax.

Every child is equally *valuable*. We can build a harmonious relationship by hugging, kissing, nurturing and comforting them. Additionally, we can create strong bonds by paying attention to them. Children are excellent teachers if we are ready to listen to them. I regularly and openly communicate with my children, and this builds a deep connection between us. When children feel loved, safe, nurtured and understood, the relationship with their parents becomes harmonious, joyful and pleasant.

Lyon is seven and Mia is ten years old now. They know that we are lot more than our bodies; they know our soul lives forever. I have taught them that we are here to learn some important lessons on Earth. We create our own reality by choosing different "positive" and "negative" experiences. When we are done with all the learning and have fulfilled our destiny, we move to another place. I've taught them how important it is to follow their passions and choose a profession they genuinely enjoy. They know how important it is to listen to their hearts and trust their intuition. They know change is good for them. They are kind, helpful, respectful and compassionate. We talk about the power of positive statements, thoughts and beliefs. They have repeated statements like, "I love myself," "I'm loved," "I can do it," "I'm worthy of the best in life" and "I'm safe" from an early age. They often create their own positive affirmations.

My children also know about the importance of regular exercise, fresh air and healthy eating. They prefer to play outdoors rather than watch television and play on their devices excessively (although they enjoy playing with them for a limited time). I find the best activities are when we combine sport with nature and fresh air such as biking, skiing, skating, playing soccer, swimming, walking and hiking.

They understand the worst negative, destructive feelings — fear, anger and hate — and the most powerful one: love. They respect and protect their environment, nature and animals. They know laughter, family and friends can help us through difficult and stressful situations. They know they don't have to be perfect or the best at everything, and it is OK to make mistakes.

They know their Guardian Angels always protect and assist them if they ask for help. Although they were initially skeptical about Angels because they can't see them, they now believe Angels truly exist, and they can turn to them for help at times. One day Mia had lost her favourite friendship necklace. She screamed and cried while we searched through her bag and pockets. Nothing. The next day she searched the classroom and asked her classmates about it. Still nothing. She called on Archangel Chamuel who helps to find lost things. Later, she saw her necklace on the teacher's desk. She was delighted. She thanked Archangel Chamuel for his help.

Lyon and Mia

They are grateful for all we have. So am I. At Thanksgiving, Mia, Lyon and I wrote a list about what we are grateful for.

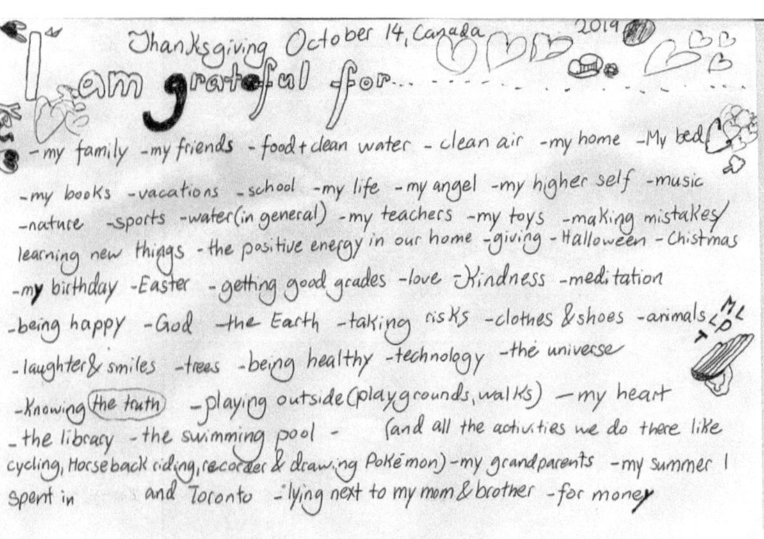

Mia's Thanksgiving List

I am thankful Thanksgiving day I am thankful
for thanksgiving. for sports?
I am thankful I am Thankful God angels
for money for my family. I am thankful
for my all my toys. I am thanful
for water I am thanful for the earth.
I am Thankful for books. I am
I am I am thanful for frer friends.
Thankful for love. I am Thanful for
laughter. I am thankful for nature.
I am thanful for air. I am thanful for fire.
I am thankful for celebrations.
I am thanful for food.
I am thanful for life. I am thankful for
seasons. I am thanful for my heart. I am thanful
for scool school. I am thakful for my soul.

Lyon's Thanksgiving List

Chapter Twelve

Post Separation: On the Way to Forgiveness

*"All the world's a stage, and all the men and
women are merely players.
They have their exits and their entrances..."*
William Shakespeare

After years of spiritual research, thinking, meditation and based on my own personal experiences, I agree with the theory that we choose every actor — spouses, parents, siblings and friends — and every event — disease, financial disaster, divorce and job loss — in our lives before we are incarnated into this body and these choices all serve the soul's evolution and spiritual growth. So, whatever lessons we came here to learn — positive and negative alike — have *a purpose* and help us grow and evolve. It also means we are responsible for our actions and have no one to blame for them. Although we don't remember why we came to Earth and what we need to learn, it can become clearer with time and awareness, as it has in my case.

We receive lots of signs — rainbows, birds, repetitive numbers, images, feathers — and messages from Angels and from the Universe along the way. We don't always recognize these signals, so we walk right by them. We only notice the big ones such as a chronic disease, a near-death experience or a life-threating accident. Sometimes we don't even notice those. Breaking my elbow was one of the messages I missed among others. It was a call to change my life, but I did nothing. A few years later, the Universe sent me more and stronger messages in the form of my diagnosis, surgeries and near-death experience; I could not dismiss them anymore.

I regularly receive signs and feel supported by the Universe. One day when I was working on my book, I looked at the time on my laptop. It showed: 11:11. Later, I was busy preparing my lunch in the kitchen. When I looked at the time on the oven's clock it was exactly 1:11. I started the dishwasher and when I checked the remaining time on the wash cycle, it read 2:22. Finally, I gazed at the time at the oven's clock before picking up my kids and it showed 2:22. I felt overwhelmed and overjoyed by the Angels' support. I saw an extraordinary phenomenon when I was walking in the park with my children one day. I looked up to the sky to witness a massive rainbow ring around the sun. The perfect circle comprised multiple colours like a rainbow with the sun exactly in the middle. A few weeks later I saw it again. I'm not sure what it means, but I take it as a stunning sign sent by the Universe.

Remember! The truth is everywhere: in songs, books, paintings and movies. Look around and you will see. Listen and you will hear. Be open to the Universe's messages and signals. Once you recognize them there is no way you can go back to your "old, unconscious life."

Life lessons can be very challenging and difficult to overcome. I asked the Angels many times: "Why do I have to face so many difficulties and challenging life situations? I've had enough." Now I know my disease and near-death experience was not a coincidence, and it happened for a reason. It was time for me to wake up and change my life. Everything that has happened in my life serves my soul's evolution and my spiritual growth. I don't believe in coincidences — I believe everything is very organized in the Universe.

It's an unfortunate fact that one must suffer emotionally, physically and mentally until we understand these lessons and change the course of our lives. *Nobody can avoid the pain in this life.* It does not matter how much money we have, how much power and influence we have or how famous we are, we still face challenges and difficulties than those less lucky, fortunate and wealthy. There is no way around it. Disease, pain, hurt, betrayal, fear, disappointment, loss of a loved one, heartbreak and old age will affect all of us.

At first this concept is difficult to accept. It seems unbelievable that it is you — your soul — who has chosen these lessons and all the "actors" and relationships in your life. It is always easier to blame others for our misfortunes. Believe me, I did it for years. My ego fought hard and persistently to keep me in the pain, anger and blame circle. When I accepted responsibility for my situations and all the "actors" in my life, forgiveness became easier. I felt lighter. I also realized that Paul has been living in pain for a long time and he projected his emotional suffering and his fears onto me.

Look around and you will find many teachers in your life who show you valuable lessons and help your soul grow. You are also a teacher who helps others around you grow spiritually. In every experience I try to find a lesson and see a teacher. I reflect on what he or she wants to teach me and why they appeared in my life. I had a few mentors help me on the way. Whenever I was ready to take the next step, the right coach, workshop, movie or book showed up — everything in perfect order and in perfect time. Whatever I had to learn was revealed to me. I tried so many techniques: hypnotherapy, reiki, spiritual retreats, Psych-K, yoga, meditation, reflexology, massage, mindfulness and acupuncture.

Margaret, a wonderful coach and spiritually awakened person has helped me with Psych-K. She guided me in changing my self-limiting beliefs in the areas of self-esteem, health and relationships. With her assistance I transformed my limiting subconscious belief system into empowering, positive beliefs. We worked a lot on establishing and increasing my self-love, self-acceptance and confidence. I now accept and love myself, and I believe I'm worthy of the best in life. Since my separation, Margaret and I have worked consistently on forgiveness for Paul and releasing all anger and resentment I had toward him and my parents. I also attended a two-day Psych-K workshop in London to learn how to create my own reality and experiences by changing my belief system.

In the summer of 2019, I attended a four-day retreat that was packed with breathing exercises, meditation, yoga, group exercises and recreational activities in nature. It was a fantastic group: eighteen like-minded people who were open to spirituality and ready to explore the true potential of our beings. We visited the ruins of an old monastery where monks once lived and worked. They had a huge library where they stored and protected ancient wisdom and knowledge. We were treated to a guided meditation while we felt the powerful energy that surrounds the place. At the Buddhist temple, we burned incense and participated in a long meditation. The temple had a peaceful, relaxing atmosphere. The next day we bathed in a lake and walked in the forest. On the last night of the retreat we had a party where we danced and sang for hours. It was one of the most memorable experiences of my life. My soul was happy and filled with peace, positive energy and joy.

In September 2019, I completed a reiki workshop in Canada. Energy healing is a powerful tool that can help us with many different issues, emotional states and resolving old traumas. I use reiki for myself and for my children.

In my opinion, the easiest and quickest way to connect to your higher self and relax your mind is through *meditation*. It has many proven benefits. At first, meditation was difficult for me: I could not focus, my attention was all over the place and my mind was flooded with many thoughts. I remained persistent and I did not give up. Focusing on my breathing and listening to the same meditation music helped me to be centred and engaged. I find it useful to have some sort of anchor for my attention. Every time the same lyrics start playing, my mind "automatically defaults" to a calm and peaceful state. This is my experience, but there are many ways to meditate. Finding your own meditation style and establishing a daily or weekly practice can be an amazing benefit. Today, meditation is integral part of my day.

Finally, I regularly use Angel Cards and Chakra Wisdom Oracle Cards for guidance and confirmation, especially when I feel stuck. Sometimes I pull out the same card repeatedly. When this happens, I pay special attention to the card's message as Angels and the Universe are trying to draw my attention to something important. All these approaches were meant to relax my mind and help me get over the negative feelings and emotions I had stored in my psyche for decades. There are many wonderful books on these and other methods. There are also plenty of groups you can join for yoga, spiritual retreat, and meditation. There is something for everyone. Try as many new different practices (safely of course) with a professional as you wish. Experiment and find what work best for you.

Through my spiritual process and practice, I reached the point when I had to let go of the past and find forgiveness in my heart. I don't know which one of the approaches ultimately helped me. It is more like a puzzle: every little piece added something until I was ready to forgive.

Chapter Thirteen

Forgiveness

"Forgiveness liberates the soul,
it removes fear.
That is why it is such a powerful weapon."
Nelson Mandela

In September 2019, I found true forgiveness in my heart for Paul. It corresponded with his request to talk about a 50-50 co-parenting arrangement. Interesting coincidence, don't you think? Or is it a coincidence? He said that he knew and felt that this was the right time to talk to me. Nonetheless I was surprised by his request, as he had repeatedly refused to accommodate the children for even a weekend since we returned to Canada. Anyhow, I agreed to meet him.

Strangely, I was excited about seeing him. After so many years of resentment, anger and hurt, I could finally meet him with an open and forgiving heart. I felt wonderful about it. My face was glowing when I entered the café. I thought there was nothing he could tell me that would upset me. I felt centred and grounded. He was already there when I arrived, so I ordered a green tea and sat down. I thought we were going to discuss the arrangement with the kids, so I listened without interrupting him. I had no idea what was coming next.

"Laura, you were right about many things," he said. "You were right to end our marriage. I was unfaithful. I was dishonest with you and uninterested in you..." and he went on and on. I listened and did not say a word for about ten minutes. Then I asked a question.

"Can we go back to the part when you said you were unfaithful? What do you mean? Where? How many times? With whom?"

I was caught completely off guard. We lived in so many different countries, and Paul travelled a lot for work. I was also often away with the kids when I visited my family at home. Was it once, twice, a few times, more? How many women? I wanted more information. Why didn't I see or suspect anything?

He told me that except for the first few years before we were married, he was cheating on me during our whole marriage in every country we lived in. It was mainly when he travelled or when I was away. He had many relationships and had sex with lots of women as he put it "too often." When he was in Central America for work for four months, he said he had a "longer" relationship. I remembered this trip. My mom helped me during those four long months while I was alone with our two very young children.

I listened to him as tears ran down my face. I wanted to stop crying but I could not control it. He had cheated on me for fourteen years. Our entire marriage. *Something collapsed within me.* I felt no anger. My soul was in pain and profound sadness. It cried somewhere deep inside me. I felt tormented, and the humiliation was overwhelming. I knew we had an unhappy marriage, but I never expected this. I could not stop crying so I went to the washroom and stayed there for few minutes. I thought I could calm down and finish our conversation, but I could not, so I decided to leave. When I arrived at home, I parked the car in the garage and stayed there for a while crying. When I got into my apartment, I began screaming and gasping for air — I could not breathe. I was hysterical and out of control for a few moments.

Hours later I was furious with Paul, so I sent him a raging email on September 20th, 2019 that made me feel better:

Paul,

You never deserved me.

Remember well what I write to you now. You will be judged for everything you have done to others and me during your lifetime. Mark my words: on the day of your passing you will feel all the pain and the humiliation I feel right now — believe me that is a lot and it feels almost unbearable — and felt during our marriage.

How could you do this to me? I almost died in the hospital. I had multiple surgeries. I was in pain after my surgeries for a long time. Then you went off to have sex with women while I was lying home and in the hospital sick, battling my disease and recovering from my surgeries. Even though I had pain, I was looking after our children or my mother while you were having your fun. What kind of person does that? You don't even understand the scale of the damage you have done.

As soon as I recovered, I did my best to meet your
sexual needs and even that was not enough for
you…

I feel sorry for you that you have been living in the
darkest of the dark places on Earth…

I wanted to tell you that I have been working on
forgiveness…

Finally, for the first time in a long time I have felt
true forgiveness in my heart for you. After what you
told me I have to start the whole process again…

Laura

He responded to my email the same day saying that he had no
excuses and he would live the rest of his life "trying to atone for
his mistakes." He also promised to tell the truth to Mia and Lyon
when they were old enough. He hoped I could forgive him one day.

I called him the next day because I wanted to hear more details
about his affairs. In our long phone conversation, he admitted
that he often felt gloomy and miserable during our marriage, and
that he was ignorant about me. He told me he couldn't live with
the guilt anymore. He kept his secrets from me for a long time
but when his lies started to eat him up, he had to share with me
everything about his affairs. The pleasure he had been seeking
over the years turned into pain he could not bear anymore. He
told me that his suffering and "paying for what he has done" had
already begun. He told me when his father passed away — Paul
was eight years old — he completely lost his faith. He said a
psychedelic mushroom experience in Amsterdam a year previous
had helped restore his faith in God and himself. Mushrooms

can heal long buried traumas and make people see things from different perspectives.

After so many years he finally heard me, and we could connect. I felt relieved and lighter after our conversation. I wanted to believe that he was a different person and had indeed changed. I thought he was going through a spiritual transformation like what I had gone through. A few days later he told the children (without getting into details) that he lied to me and apologized. Finally, he had taken responsibility for what he did and talked to our children about our marriage. It was a long overdue conversation. He also committed to helping the children and me more in the future.

A few days later, I met Margaret and told her what happened. I stayed calm while talking about Paul's affairs and his betrayal. I was so surprised by my own reaction. I was not upset at all and did not understand what was going on.

Why am I not angry? I thought.

I should be angry; I felt I should take revenge on him and make him pay for all the pain he caused me. Then I realized I didn't want those things. It was my ego that wanted to retaliate and avenge my humiliation. It was my ego that wanted to fight. My heart and soul wanted peace and a calm relationship with the father of my children. Margaret explained that it is only the soul that can react like this. She told me I had just taken "an evolutionary step" in my soul's journey.

A week later, Paul and I had a long conversation about the children. He had missed a lot, so I told him what had happened since we arrived in Canada. I also shared my confused feelings about him. He said he didn't expect love or forgiveness or anything from me, but "he was open to anything."

What if he really changed and he is the person I always wanted? I thought. Do we have a chance together in the future? Maybe in a few years? Negative thoughts filled my mind: my anger returned, and my ego took control. I was upset with myself for even thinking about rekindling our relationship.

I wanted more details about his affairs, so I asked him about them again. He sent me a text message on October 3rd, 2019 saying that I was a beautiful, strong and incredible woman. He complimented me on being a good mother and how compassionate I am. He was sorry for betraying me and for the pain he caused. He told me he still loved me, and that he was very confused and weak. He wished he could turn back time and change everything. In his next text message, he said we were both different people now. He wanted two happy and healthy parents to raise our children. He said that laughter and joy could heal our lives instead of focusing of the past.

I told him he had to live with himself and what he had done. "We" does not exist, I said. "It's only you and me and the children." In a subsequent email sent to him on October 4th, 2019, I said: We have nothing left to discuss. Just to be clear again: I never ever in this world want anything from you other than a normal and respectful relationship for our children's sake. Wake up! Think! I divorced you before I knew about your betrayal. So it was bad enough. Forgiveness does not mean I will ever want to have a relationship with you!

Once again, I was full of anger and my ego was ready to seek revenge. I needed to release these negative emotions before working toward forgiveness in my heart. In a way, I resisted forgiveness. My ego convinced me that it is not normal to forgive someone a few days after they reveal they betrayed you and lied to you for over a decade.

As Tolle put it in *The Power of Now* (2004), it is crucial to be present in the now. If we are not present in the moment and our mind is constantly preoccupied with the past, this can result in "all forms of non-forgiveness" such as guilt, remorse, resentment, disappointment, anger and sorrow (p. 61). That is exactly what happened to me.

I had been living in the past and the future far too long, and I was ready to let go of all the negativity I carried for years. I was prepared to live in the present. I didn't want any more drama in my life. All I wanted was peace, joy and love inside and around me. I wanted to be surrounded by loving, kind and happy people.

Forgiveness was the key to achieving all of this.

I asked for the Angels' help to find true forgiveness for Paul in my heart once again. They told me, "You shouldn't ask for what you already have. You already forgave him before you met him." It was true. I went to meet him with true forgiveness in my heart. Even though he told me something shocking, I could not be angry with him.

> "Is there anything else I can do?" I asked my Angels.

> "Send him love," they said.

So I did. I closed my eyes and, in my meditative state of mind, I sent him love.

Paul tried to convince me that we still had a future together while I was claiming we didn't. He couldn't accept what I explained to him several times: that forgiving does not mean that I want to have an intimate relationship with him ever again. It went on for weeks. The more he pressured me, the more I pushed back. After ten months apart, I think he realized what he had lost and how empty his life was. Since he was on a spiritual journey, his priorities might have changed. Money, a career, sex, expensive suits and luxury vacations were being replaced by more meaningful values like spending time with his children and letting go of his anger.

He was desperate to restore our relationship and return to the "known" and the comfort he had for years. On the other hand, he was looking for someone else. I knew this because I came across his profile on two different online dating websites where I was also registered. I believe he was confused and struggling between his old and new lives. On October 21th 2019 he sent me a text message saying if it took several lifetimes to make it up to me, he would. He said he wanted to demonstrate to the kids that miracles are possible. He also wanted to prove that he is the man I'm searching for. He texted me that he was sorry for not loving me more when he had a chance. He finished his text message with: "There is always hope."

I believe his clinging to get his old life back was another of his ego's games. It wasn't love but a desperate attempt to prove to me and his children that he was a different person. It was another manipulation. He told me that he would "wait" for me, so I made it clear that I didn't want him to wait for me nor did I want to give him false hope. It annoyed me how pushy he was, and I wondered why he wouldn't let me alone. I was angry at him once again.

I needed to find the right balance with him, so I kept my distance and communicated with him as little as possible. He needed to understand that my kindness did not mean a second chance between us. On the other hand, I did not want to be rude to him. I wanted to stay forgiving and compassionate in my heart toward him, which was challenging. Occasionally it was lot harder than I imagined. Even though he tried to restore our relationship, I know that our separation has changed his life for the better: he now meditates and exercises regularly. He changed his diet and spends more quality time with our children. I hope he finds his peace and happiness. I like everything in my life as it is right now. It is perfect and I have no intention of going back to him or my old life.

After almost a year apart, we had our first family lunch together at Thanksgiving. Everybody had a great time eating a delicious four-course homemade meal. After lunch, I had another conversation with Paul where I was a little distant with him. He admitted that he always thought I was "the weak one" and he was "the strong one" in our marriage. He realized that was not true; everything I had gone through alone proved that I'm very strong.

When Paul dropped off the kids a few days after our Thanksgiving lunch, I hugged him. I knew it would happen one day when I was ready, and that was the day. After a year, that hug felt extraordinary. Mia said, "This is impossible." Then she and Lyon also hugged us. Hugs have a powerful impact on people's lives — the person who is ready to forgive and the person who needs forgiveness. I recognize now that Paul has taught me the valuable lesson of forgiveness. As strange as it sounds, forgiving him was "easier" than forgiving myself. Marrying and loving someone who hurt me so deeply for such a long period of time was tough to forgive. It was also difficult to understand why I did not end my marriage sooner. I had to forgive myself so I could be free.

We went "trick or treating" together with the children at Halloween. The kids had so much fun collecting candies from house to house, and we enjoyed watching them. The kids spent the first week of Christmas holidays with me. We played board games and went for long walks in the snow along the frozen river every day. We had a wonderful Christmas dinner with my cousin's family at my place. It was one of the most relaxing and peaceful Christmas seasons since my childhood holidays I remember so fondly. Mia and Lyon spent the second week with Paul and his family. Paul is now more involved in raising our kids than ever before and is now willing to accommodate the children two nights a month.

At Easter (in 2020) we had another family lunch. It was so interesting to see everything from a different perspective as an "observer". When I looked at Paul, I had an odd feeling. It almost felt surreal that I spent seventeen years with this man. He was so "strange" to me. It was like looking at him with different eyes.

Our relationship as a couple has ended. Now we have a different relationship — a partnership to raise two children together by sharing parental responsibilities and focusing on the children's best interests and well-being.

During the first year after my separation many wonderful changes happened to me; it was one of the most eventful and exciting years of my life. *I did it.* I did everything I wanted, and I regained power over my life. After so many years I'm connected to my higher self and I feel *alive* again. I don't have to prove to anyone that I'm *worthy*. I know I am. I feel strong, confident, happy, and beautiful inside and out.

Conclusion

What I have shared with you is the past. It is done and cannot be changed. If there is one thing I learned from this experience, it's that the more you talk about your problems and the people who hurt and betrayed you, the more you relive that experience and the worse you feel. Why suffer and torture yourself? I did it for years. I complained about my relationship and I shared my problems over and over again with friends and family. Did it help? Did I feel better? No. If anything I felt worse.

Today I accept responsibility for all that happened to me without blaming anyone. As strange as it sounds, I feel grateful for my disease and my near-death experience because they woke me up and put me on a spiritual fast track. I'm also thankful for my negative experiences during my marriage. As painful as they were, they taught me the important lesson of forgiveness. In addition, I have received a precious gift, a blessing: my two children. All the challenging experiences during my move and the separation have empowered me and made my soul evolve. Finally, the pain and humiliation during my marriage and divorce eventually led me to my life's purpose.

I had been looking for my spiritual purpose, my "Personal Legend,"[5] unsuccessfully since 2015. Paulo Coelho used the concept of Personal Legend in his book, the Alchemist. According to *The IQ Matrix*, a blog I read,

> "A Personal Legend is your life's spiritual purpose.
> It's a spiritual calling that awakens a deep desire
> and passion to live with a sense of purpose for
> something greater than yourself."[6]

Sometimes I became frustrated and impatient, so I asked my Angels, "Why can't you help me and show me why I'm here? I know I have a purpose only I don't remember it." I always knew and felt deep down that my purpose was to help other human beings and increase human consciousness; I just did not know how or what to do.

The evening I started to read *The Alchemist* I asked the Angels and the Universe to reveal the purpose of my life in my dreams. I remember looking for it all night, but I did not remember anything the next morning. I was very disappointed. So, I told my Angels and my higher self during meditation: "I have been searching for my spiritual purpose for years. Please help me. Please show me." At last, it was revealed to me: I have to write a book about my life. The next thought was the book's title: *Forgiveness*. At the age of forty-one, I have found a great treasure on Earth: my destiny.

---

[5] Paulo Coelho: The Alchemist, Harper One and Harper Collins, 2014

[6] Source: Adam Sicinski: https://blog.iqmatrix.com/personal-legend. Accessed on June 18, 2020

Once I realized what it was, I became enthusiastic and motivated beyond words, and felt deep down that I was now able to help others through fulfilling my destiny. Although the road toward completing my destiny was rocky and full of challenges, I did not give up because I knew in my heart that I had to do it.

This book is my Personal Legend. My life's spiritual purpose.

My message to you is to forgive. Forgiveness is the key to your freedom and inner peace. No matter how hard, desperate, or hopeless your situation is, there is always a way out. All you have to do is to get rid of fear. Ask and trust yourself and the Universe, God/Goddess, Angels, your higher self, your inner voice, your feelings and intuition. Let your spirit guide you.

Believe in yourself! Believe that you are powerful, valuable and significant. The majority of people think of themselves as insignificant and helpless to change anything in this world. How wrong they are. *Every thought and action* — even the smallest decision — *impacts other people's lives.* Every little change can make a huge difference in your life and in the lives around you. We are all connected and dependent on each other more than we are aware of.

I have known my other life purposes for a long time:

- ◆ Help as many people as I can in my lifetime
- ◆ Spread love and kindness
- ◆ Raise my children in a very conscious way

After sharing all the knowledge and wisdom I gained, my grown-up children can help fellow human beings in the process of awakening and creating a better world based on equality, fairness, kindness, forgiveness, peace, love and protecting nature and animals.

It is also important to let go of the old and welcome new in your life. The only way is to make space for the new by letting go of the old. Remember to follow your dreams and your passions. Be open to change and new experiences because these can help you grow. Let go of the fear that holds you back from reaching your true potential and the fulfillment of your destiny. Remember to live in the present instead of planning your future and struggling with your past. Most importantly: love yourself. You are never alone! You are always supported.

When you leave this world, all that matters is your *heart*. Help as many people as you can on your way. Be kind, loving and compassionate. You won't take your car, house, job, possessions, bank accounts, money, jewelry with you, so try to live your life by the highest standard of love, forgiveness and kindness.

While I was finishing my book, humanity was given an extraordinary opportunity to "look deeper within" during the coronavirus pandemic. Millions of people have been ordered to stay home, follow social distancing, measures and in some cases self-isolate or quarantine. Never before have these many people been forced to stay home and slow down. Schools, retail stores, pubs and restaurants are closed. Most people are working from home. Basically, everything is closed worldwide; only essential services and hospitals are running at full capacity. Our old way of life is being challenged. It's like we are being forced to slow down and take a break from our chaotic routines. This is a marvelous opportunity to connect with your higher self and the Universe.

Understandably, for most people these changes have been profound and distressing; for a small group of people, including myself, it is an adjustment. Although my children are home every day and we have our challenges — like online learning and keeping two active children busy in a small apartment — we manage it and adjust to the new circumstances. The positive impact of the pandemic is that I spend more quality time with my kids, which has resulted in a deeper connection between us. For the first time, Mia and I did an online yoga class together then went for a run along the river. We go biking, walking and explore new parks and streets in our neighbourhood. My children and I enjoy the fresh air, green trees and beautiful sunshine every day. I also decided to resume one of my old passions: photography.

This is the perfect time to ask some of the questions I listed earlier, make a list of goals and re-evaluate your life. It is also a great opportunity to meditate, connect with universal consciousness, and spend more time outdoors. Many people will go back to the "known" and continue living their lives as before and that is OK. On the other hand, there will be people who will question their automated lives and make significant changes and conscious choices. Nobody knows yet how long these restrictions will last. The more important question to ask is how our lives will change at the end of this global epidemic. Do we go back to *our old way of life* based on conflict and competition and focused on material possessions? Or do we choose a *new way of life* that is more aligned with our spirits and founded on cooperation, kindness and mutual respect?

During my spiritual voyage I have unlocked tremendous potential within myself that I was unaware of. Divorcing and moving to another country as a single mom with two kids was inconceivable for me before. Equally, writing a memoir with spiritual truths in a language other than my mother tongue was unimaginable. Publishing my book required lots of courage and determination. Finally, expressing my truth and sharing my story with the world have empowered me. I tapped into something unexplainable and so powerful it is difficult to grasp with the mind. By the time this book will be published in the summer of 2020 I will have reached two important milestones: the five-year mark of my diagnosis (all of my test results are good) and the five-year anniversary of the beginning of my spiritual journey. Although this amount of time is merely "a drop in the ocean" of the Universe's infinite and timeless vastness, it has been long enough to affect my life in an extraordinary way.

My life is complete, whole and perfect. I'm free, strong, independent, relaxed, confident and happy. I value my freedom immensely. I create my own experiences, take responsibility for my life and appreciate small wonders in my everyday.

We don't need lots of money to accomplish these wonders; they are available to everyone. Discover small miracles in your everyday life! You can write your own gratitude list. I'll share some of the miracles I've experienced in the last year that I'm grateful for:

Sitting in the sand and meditating under the sky at a nearby lake
Eating my homemade banana bread with a cup of green tea
Good laughter with my kids when my son makes a joke
Biking on a beautiful tree-lined path along the lake
Dancing a night through with "strangers" in a club
Walking while watching the beautiful falling leaves
Lying in bed next to my daughter and my son
Having dinner with friends and family
Kissing and making love passionately
Skating in the sunshine
Reading a good book
Going out on a date
Having a massage
Hugging someone
Smiling at someone
Skiing in the mountains
Watching a funny movie
Exercising in a group class
Connecting with new people
Trick or treating with my children
Taking photos of birds and nature
Writing and publishing my book
Swimming in the pool and in the lake
Listening to music and singing loudly
Enjoying my morning coffee with a muffin
Feeling relaxed and peaceful after my yoga practice
Walking to school with my children in the magical snowfall
Dancing in "ecstasy" in my living room in front of the mirror

Changing my life has been hard work. It has taken me years to get where I am right now. Moreover, I still have lots of work ahead of me. I have new goals and different challenges now, but I continue investing significant energy and considerable time into my new lifestyle: I spend lots of time cooking my healthy meals, exercising, meditating and connecting to nature. Most importantly, I'm raising my two children as a single mom the best I can.

One new goal is to find a fulfilling and meaningful job where I can be in service to others. Another goal is to continue working on my happiness and my inner peace, which does not depend on another person or circumstances but only me. In other words, I want to stay connected to my higher self and the Universe. I'm also working toward transcending my ego, which sometimes manifests in frustration and impatience. Finally, I aim to increase my vibration, and raise my energy and access to my feminine power. It is important for me to remain balanced and calm even if something goes "wrong" or not in a way I planned. As we all know, this often happens so it is a continuous challenge.

I have difficult days and I will continue to have challenges as long as I'm here. Life throws more challenges in various forms: a difficult person or unexpected bills, a frustrating and long job search, disease, a tough business negotiation or conflict with my children just to name few. Yet I have to deal with them every day. I create my own experiences every day, every hour and every minute of my life. So do you. You are the creator of your life and your experiences.

Rebuilding my life and restoring my physical, emotional and mental health was a "full-time job". It took considerable time and required tremendous inner strength, determination, persistence, and practice. Do I want to go back? Never! I enjoy my new life as a single mom, I evolve every day, and I look forward to new exciting and fun experiences. Life is the biggest adventure if we make it so.

Every day I make a conscious effort to live my life without regrets. I want to make sure I have done everything I wanted to, desired and planned for in this journey on Earth. Living my life and dying without regrets while being true to myself are the biggest gifts I can give myself. So can you.

My journey in this body on Earth will end one day,
but my soul's journey will never end.
It goes on forever.

I know who I AM and why I AM here.

I am AWARE and I am CONSCIOUS.

I am FREE.

References

- Eckhart Tolle: *The Power of Now*, New World Library, Namaste Publishing, 2004
- David Servan-Schreiber, M.D., Ph.D.: *Anticancer, A New Way of Life*, Collins, HarperCollins Publisher Ltd, 2008
- Louise Hay: *You Can Heal Your Life*, Hay House, 1984
- Paulo Coelho: *The Alchemist, 25th Anniversary Edition*, Harper One and HarperCollins, 2014
- Sogyal Rinpoche: *The Tibetan Book of Living and Dying*, HarperCollins, 2002
- Online resource:
  Adam Sicinski: IQ Matrix: https://blog.iqmatrix.com/personal-legend

Online resources

- GAIA: https://www.gaia.com/ - Great variety of movies, huge selection of documentaries, series, yoga practices, meditation and recipes

Bibliography

- Abby Wynne: *Energy Healing*, Hay House, 2015
- Christopher Hansard: *The Tibetan Art of Living*, Atria Books, 2003
- Christopher Hansard: *The Tibetan Art of Serenity*, Hodder Paperback, 2007
- David Servan-Schreiber, M.D., Ph.D.: *Anticancer, A New Way of Life*, Collins, HarperCollins Publisher Ltd, 2008
- Deepak Chopra: *Life After Death*, Three Rivers Press, 2006
- Deepak Chopra: *The Seven Spiritual Laws of Success*, Amber-Allen Publishing, 1994
- Doreen Virtue: *10 Messages Your Angels Want You to Know*, Hay House, 2017
- Doreen Virtue: *Healing with the Angels Oracle Cards*, Hay House, 1999
- Doreen Virtue: *Healing with the Angels*, Hay House, 1999
- Doreen Virtue: *The Angel Therapy Handbook*, Hay House, 2012
- Eben Alexander, M.D.: *Proof of Heaven*, Simon & Schuster Paperbacks, 2012
- Eckhart Tolle: *The Power of Now*, New World Library, Namaste Publishing, 2004
- Esther and Jerry Hicks: *Ask and It Is Given*, Hay House, 2004

- Gabrielle Bernstein: *Miracles Now – 108 Life-Changing Tools for Less Stress, More Flow, and Finding Your True Purpose*, Hay House, 2014
- Ian Gawler: *You Can Conquer Cancer – A New Way of Living*, Penguin Group, 1986
- Lissa Rankin, M.D.: *The Fear Cure*, Hay House, 2015
- Lorna Byrne: *Angels at My Fingertips*, Coronet, 2017
- Louise Hay: *Life! Reflections on Your Journey*, Hay House, 1995
- Louise Hay: *Meditations to Heal Your Life*, Hay House, 1994
- Louise Hay: *You Can Heal Your Life*, Hay House, 1984
- Neale Donald Walsch: *Conversations with God Book 1*, Hodder & Stoughton, 1995
- Neale Donald Walsch: *Conversations with God Book 2*, Hodder & Stoughton, 1997
- Neale Donald Walsch: *Conversations with God Book 3*, Hodder & Stoughton, 1998
- Paulo Coelho: *The Alchemist, 25th Anniversary Edition*, Harper One and HarperCollins, 2014
- Richard Béliveau, Ph.D., and Denis Gingras, Ph.D.: *Foods that Fight Cancer – Preventing Cancer Through Diet*, McClelland & Stewart Ltd., 2005
- Sally Kempton: *Awakening Shakti, The Transformative Power of the Goddesses of Yoga*, Sounds True, 2013
- Shamash Alidina: *The Mindful Way Through Stress*, The Guilford Press, 2015
- Sogyal Rinpoche: *The Tibetan Book of Living and Dying*, HarperCollins, 2002
- T. Colin Campbell, PhD and Thomas M. Campbell II, MD: *The China Study*, BenBella Books, 2006
- Tori Hartman: *Chakra Wisdom Oracle Cards and Guidebook*, Watkins Publishing, 2014
- Tricia McCannon: *The Angelic Origins of the Soul*, Bear & Company, 2017